- You can return this item to any Bournemouth library but not all libraries are open every day.

- Items must be returned on or before the due date. Please note that you will be charged for items returned late.

- Items may be renewed unless requested by another customer.

- Renewals can be made in any library, by telephone, email or online via the website. Your membership card number and PIN will be required.

- Please look after this item - you may be charged for any damage.

Bournemouth
Libraries

www.bournemouth.gov.uk/libraries

AROUND WALES

BY B-ROADS AND BYWAYS

AROUND WALES

BY B-ROADS AND BYWAYS

Jamie Owen

EBURY
PRESS

For my friends and family

Contents

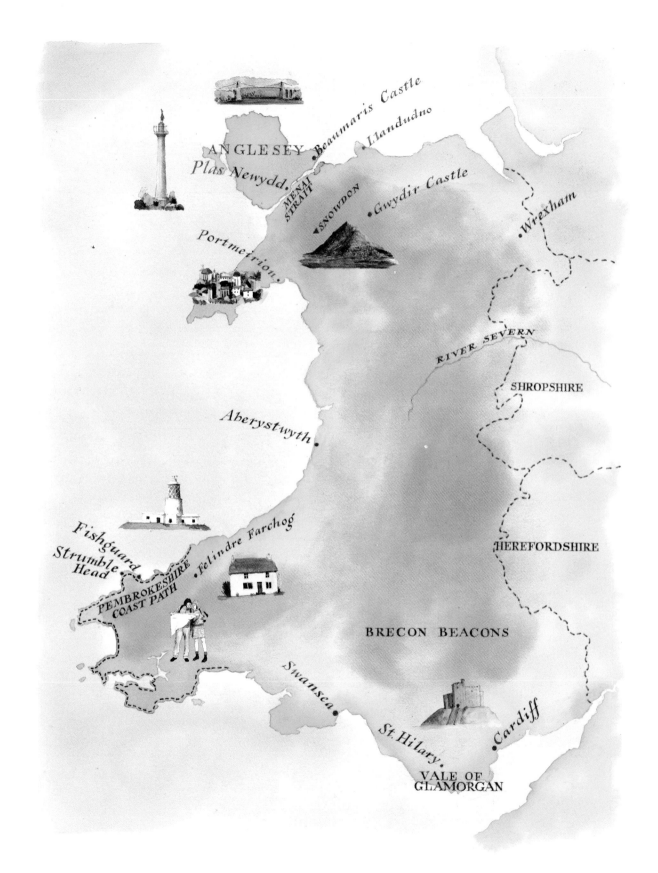

ANGLESEY

Beaumaris Castle

Llandudno

Plas Newydd

MENAI STRAIT

Snowdon

Gwydir Castle

Wrexham

Portmeirion

RIVER SEVERN

SHROPSHIRE

Aberystwyth

Fishguard

Strumble
Head

Felindre Farchog

HEREFORDSHIRE

PEMBROKESHIRE
COAST PATH

BRECON BEACONS

Swansea

St. Hilary

Cardiff

VALE OF
GLAMORGAN

Introduction

WHY BOTHER exploring Wales when it is so easy to jump on a plane and travel to any other corner of the world? It's a question I was asked many times in the year of weekends and holidays that I spent travelling around the country in writing this book. The answer is simple. It is my home: it is where I was born, where I grew up with my two brothers and where I now work. Though I am a child of the package holiday generation, my family never really did the foreign beach fortnight. My parents reasoned that living on the coast in Pembrokeshire nowhere else in the world would ever really match up. Holidays were instead spent exploring the local area, and this fostered in me an abiding love of the countryside. We three boys were never bored – there was always another lane to cycle down or another beach to wander across. Wherever I've lived since then, I've felt an overwhelming yearning to return again and again to the Welsh countryside.

ABOVE: *Writing notes at the foot of Snowdon*

BELOW: *My family. My brother Richard, Mum, me, Dad and my brother Huw*

Though Wales is a small country, it is a diverse one with most of its treasures well hidden. It is this that prompted my most recent journeys around this country. I began one November, and over the next ten months I spent many long weekends wandering around this often misunderstood part of the United Kingdom. 'For Wales see England' is how some early travel books dealt with the country – and among nineteenth-century travel books that was one of the more sympathetic entries. That attitude couldn't be further from the truth these days. Not only does Wales have a certain spring in its step, particularly since gaining a degree of autonomy, but there is also a growing fashion for rediscovering the simple pleasures of climbing over a castle and rambling through the countryside – both of which Wales has in spades.

When it came to choosing the areas to visit, I headed first for Pembrokeshire, my home county, though to the less familiar northern side. After that invigorating trek around

the coast, I toured Cardiff, a city laden with history that has reinvented itself (with huge success) in the past few years, before moving on to a little-appreciated part of the country, the Vale of Glamorgan. Next I headed north to tackle Anglesey, then worked my way round from Llandudno to Portmeirion (diverting to agricultural shows and ghost-ridden manors); and then finally I climbed to the summit of Snowdon. Along the way I visited the birthplace of William Morgan, admired the architecture of Sir Clough Williams-Ellis, marvelled at the rugged coastline of North Pembrokeshire, wandered wide-eyed through some of the country's most beautiful houses and gardens, and soaked up the scenery in a destination that must surely rank as among the most beautiful in Europe.

As the title suggests, most of this was achieved using only B-roads and byways. This isn't perhaps as difficult as it sounds in Wales – after all, we have only one stretch of motorway – but in any case B-roads have a certain romance to them. I also wanted to walk as much of the countryside as possible. As a child I walked to school and my weekends always ended up striding along a windswept beach. As someone who now spends much of my life hunched over a desk I yearn for the days off when I pull on my boots and set out in search of solitude.

This, then, is the record of my jaunts, part travel guide, part history book, part personal musings on the changing landscape of Wales. There are inevitably some omissions of places I would like to have visited had I had all the time in the world; these I now keep filed away at the back of my mind, waiting for the next free weekend. For every view cherished another goes by unnoticed and ignored until another wander beckons.

ABOVE: *The Pembrokeshire cottage where I stayed while walking the coast path.*

BELOW: *Family day out in North Pembrokeshire*

OPPOSITE: *Gwydir Castle*

Chapter One

The Pembrokeshire Coast Path (Part I)

POPPIT SANDS ❂ ST DOGMAELS ❂ CEMAES HEAD ❂
CEIBWR BAY ❂ MOYLGROVE ❂ PWLL Y WRACH ❂
NEWPORT

*I*T'S A freezing cold Saturday morning in November, and I'm standing bleary-eyed at the start of one of the great walks of Britain – the Pembrokeshire Coast Path. One hundred and eighty-six miles of some of the world's most stunning coastline begins here and ends on the other side of the county, in Amroth. The Pembrokeshire coast was designated a National Park in the austerity of the 1950s because it's home to virtually every type of geological landform found in the UK. The path itself opened nearly twenty years later. It couldn't have been easy persuading hundreds of landowners to let the great unwashed tramp along the edge of their land. The thought of hikers leaving gates open and lighting bonfires must have traumatized Pembrokeshire's landed families, even though countryside lovers tend in the main to be quite civilized types.

OPPOSITE: The remarkable rock formations at Cemaes Head viewed from high on the coast path.

Most people in Pembrokeshire (and I include myself in this as one who was born here) are inordinately proud of the National Park. It's everyone's playground, a place to explore after school, play in the holidays and walk the dog. I spent my childhood weekends on the beaches in the south of the county, and all of my life I have walked the same short stretches over and over again. However, I've never explored much of the north coast. That is about to change. For years I've been promising myself that I would walk the long stretch from St Dogmaels to Strumble Head and this morning is the start of a couple of days of exploring. It's 15 miles of pretty tough hiking to my overnight stop in Newport. I walk fairly often but I'm no exercise freak, so this is a bit more than my usual Sunday constitutional.

The Pembrokeshire Coast National Park is one of the smallest in Britain and the only coastal National Park. I don't know what I'd expected to see at the starting point – maybe a statue or a visitors' centre. Elsewhere, there'd be a glass dome inviting me to enjoy 'The Coastal Experience' – instead, blink and you'd miss the low plinth in the corner of the car park marking the start of the route. It's all understated, very Welsh, almost apologetic. The ribbon was cut on 16 May 1970 by the great BBC war correspondent Wynford Vaughan-Thomas. It may not have been the

---

WYNFORD VAUGHAN-THOMAS

I've just worked on a documentary about Wynford Vaughan-Thomas's life and the script is still fresh in my mind. To my parents' and grandparents' generations he was the great BBC wartime radio correspondent and the commentator in hushed tones at the coronations of George VI and then the Queen. We grew up watching his adventures on the TV as he travelled around his beloved country in his later years. He grew up in Swansea, went to Oxford, witnessed the deprivation during the depression of the South Wales Valleys in 1930s, joined the BBC, made historic radio broadcasts from D-Day beaches and a bomber over Berlin, and then witnessed the results of the atrocities of Belsen and Auschwitz. All of his life he'd sought solace in the Welsh countryside and as a kid coming home from school I remember seeing him on the box in his dotage – this fanatical old professor-type character making documentaries about steam railways or climbing Snowdon. He was mesmerizing and inspiring.

---

most momentous of world events that year (in which Colonel Gaddafi took over as Libya's premier, Ted Heath beat Harold Wilson to Downing Street and a state of emergency was called over Britain's dock strike), but in Pembrokeshire this modest opening ceremony marked the birth of one of Wales's greatest tourism treasures and was headline news.

Today, in the same car park where Wynford Vaughan-Thomas had once stood, there's just a naked surfer taking too long to change outside his car, and me. I wanted to come here in the middle of winter when the crowds had gone. I know Pembrokeshire's seasons well and know too that July and August (when it's likely to be raining) will see hordes fill this car park. But at this time of year the lanes will be empty and the countryside mine. If I'm very lucky the sun will shine now and then.

St Dogmaels

The first village I come across is St Dogmaels, a pretty place of stone terraces and narrow streets that once the holiday season has ended can breathe again, freed of summer traffic. The visitors come to see the ruins of the Abbey, and the nearby water mill, Y Felin. One of only two medieval water mills still working in Wales, it is thought to have been built by the monks in the twelfth century. Some come here to play on the estuary and a few determined souls park here and start the odyssey of the coastal walk.

Long before Wynford's visit, the Vikings came to St Dogmaels Abbey and as – they so often did when they dropped in on quiet, peace-loving communities – sacked it. I often wonder what period of history people have in mind when they talk fondly about the 'good old days'. Later those wholesome Benedictine monks (who knew a good location when they saw one) established themselves here in 1115 under the patronage of Robert Martyn, Lord of Cemaes. The Black Death came to this part of Pembrokeshire in 1349, and over time the number of monks dwindled, but in the end it was Henry VIII's Dissolution of the Monasteries in 1536 that pretty much did for St Dogmaels Abbey. There isn't much left of the building now but the surviving carving of a flower on the north door gives an inkling of the wealth and beauty of what stood here nearly 800 years ago.

It's sleepy and quiet here, and miles from anywhere really (although in reality Cardiff's only a three-hour drive away). For a few lucky souls this is picturesque home, a quaint stone village with a view of the sea. A good few of these houses are empty holiday homes, however: St Dogmaels is too far from the big cities. This is the end of Britain, the westerly extremities of Wales where the fields fall into the water. But when the sea was the main thoroughfare for goods and passengers, this place and the Welsh coast marked the gateway to the world.

St Dogmaels parish church houses the famous Sagranus Stone. Inscribed in Latin and the Ogham language, it provided the key to the interpretation of the Ogham alphabet that had mystified scholars until 1848. I could spend the day strolling around the narrow roads but the coast calls and it's already going to be a darker end to the day than I'd planned.

The picturesque village of St Dogmaels, with the ruined abbey in the foreground.

It's low tide and the sandbanks are stretched out trying to dry in the weak sun. This is the end of the River Teifi after tumbling downhill for 75 miles from its source 1500 feet above sea level in the Cambrian

Mountains. Its last duty before washing into the sea is to mark the boundary between the counties of Ceredigion and Pembrokeshire. A small flotilla of boats is lined up on moorings to watch the incoming tide; older abandoned vessels lie stranded above high water in reeds on the foreshore, like grandparents watching children on the beach, too wobbly themselves to brave the surf.

Off the far headland, the worst of the Atlantic's rollers punch the nose of Cardigan Island. The white rush of water is spectacular to watch even from here, though it's too far to hear the waves crashing on the rocks. Pembrokeshire is the first landfall for the clouds and waves that have been blown and rolled thousands of miles across the Atlantic. When the storms hit these headlands their brutality is terrific. Carmarthenshire, further inland, hides behind Pembrokeshire, watching through her hands while the worst of nature's temper is meted out on her neighbour.

Good grief, I'm unfit. I remember watching Wynford climbing Snowdon on the TV and thinking that the rather portly elderly explorer might have a heart attack on screen, such was his panting. The hill up to Cemaes Head is steep; at least, that's my excuse for sweating. I've got my walking boots on; my rucksack is loaded with waterproof jacket and trousers, woolly hat, water, food, Brian John's guidebook and the Ordnance Survey map of North Pembrokeshire. As soon as I began walking I knew I had packed too much. It's cool, dry and (when the sun dares to show) almost warm, for November anyway. They seem to have got the weather forecast wrong too – I've prepared for a monsoon.

The hedgerows are still yellow with gorse in full bloom, but its usual pungent scent has been lost with the summer and diluted by the frequent rain. Between the fence posts, confused clumps of disorganized pink campions reach out for sunlight. The fields are like an old watercolour, the once dazzling bold colours of May and June now faded and bleached, only an impression of greater things past.

Stretching up the hill, there's a raggle-taggle of cottages with spectacular views across the bay. Many of them are empty and cold, waiting for a booking. I don't know what it is that immediately identifies a holiday cottage; perhaps it's the lack of the usual detritus of human life (no bulging refuse sacks, no milk bottles or embarrassing washing drying on the line). Across the water in Gwbert, a huge hotel keeps watch over the ocean. It's out of scale with the houses sharing its road and looks forbidding – a concrete fortress too brutal for such a beautiful perch. But that is the story of Britain generally and Wales in particular: take a piece of paradise and then plonk something

A CAPTIVATING FIND

Just over the fence in the shallows of the estuary's mouth, archaeologists searching satellite images have found what appears to be an enormous thousand-year-old fish trap built from stone in the shape of a 'V'. They think it was designed to catch migratory fish such as salmon and sea trout swimming up the River Teifi. It is a substantial construction and may have been heaved into position when sea levels were lower

than today's. Dyfed Archaeological Trust's divers have examined the trap and found it covered in worms, algae and sea anemones. Over the past millennium it has metamorphosed from a man-made structure into a natural reef. They're continuing their research to firm up their findings but there's a small part of me that rather hopes that our ancestors constructed a giant V in the water simply as an ageless gesture of defiance.

ugly on top of it. Yet the Welsh are a quiet people and grateful too – we don't like to make a fuss when something aesthetically hideous blights our lives.

Until I stop walking I feel not just warm but hot. There's a gate at the top of the hill overlooking Cemaes Head, so I sit there for a moment to look back at the view. A vast black cloud blurs the horizon and the sky – heavy, cold and unkind, it's one of those storms that has raced across the ocean and is ready to drop its rain like bombs. It's not easy to judge when it might arrive – perhaps in a few hours, perhaps tomorrow.

Until now the path has been well made and hard surfaced – and almost entirely uphill. Now, however, I have reached the end of the tarmac road, and have begun to go downhill on a deteriorating gravel path. In the distance is a scruffy, dirty-cream farm and opposite it, across in a field, a large man-made pond. A new and substantial fence has been built recently to keep something out of (or perhaps in) its whiffy, still waters. Approaching the building, there's no name on the gate but this is an animal sanctuary of some sort, run for the benefit of its inmates rather than for visitors. A collection box placed on a post half-heartedly appeals to the few passing walkers. The owners might be asleep or away but the handful of well-fed ponies, ducks and chickens are enjoying the peace and the view. A seriously fat rabbit makes me jump when it raises its head above the long grass. It fixes me with a stare and shows none of the usual rabbit-like tendency to run away. In the middle of the right-of-way, the house's outbuildings keep guard over a lifetime's rusting tin cans. This place is beyond the sweep of the county's refuse collection, so the time-honoured Pembrokeshire tradition of religiously piling up rubbish is observed. Beyond the gate a prehistoric Land Rover lies half in the hedge, the long grass growing up through its disappearing floor.

I want to slow down and peek through the windows of the house but can't be sure that there is no one at home. One unusual thing about the Coast Path is the way it nosily meanders though many private front gardens and past many kitchen windows – and is all the more delightful for that. I assume that no one would leave a white rabbit outside to fend for itself, so someone must be home somewhere.

Towards Cemaes Head

I'm making good progress as I stride towards Careg Lydan and Careg Aderyn, straddling the next stretch of the coast path to Cemaes Head. The trees touch together at their tops to form an arch. Crippled and twisted by gales from birth, November has yet to blast their dying canopy of leaves from late gold to yellow then baldness – though judging by the gathering breeze, this might be their last weekend of full plumage.

Cemaes Head, now coming into view, is the most northerly of the headlands of the Pembrokeshire coast. At 550 feet it's also home to some of county's highest cliffs. It's battered by the full force of the Atlantic, and everything that lives on it or around it is shaped by the howling weather. In North Pembrokeshire staying short is the key to surviving the lashing wind. Where the stunted trees and their twisted branches give up on the land, bell heather, western gorse and rusted bracken run riot across the earth. For all its seeming wildness, however, this is a managed landscape. Welsh Mountain Ponies have been reintroduced here to tramp down the bracken to encourage the breeding of choughs (a bird related to the crow). Four ponies stop chewing for a moment to look up at their passing visitor but then return their slathering mouths to the ground.

PEMBROKESHIRE COTTAGES

*T*he farmhouses around here remind me of my grandparents' isolated cottage on the other side of the county – poor Pembrokeshire stone walls rendered with rough cement that never kept out the rain, all under a low Welsh slate roof. There was no central heating – whatever the weather, the Rayburn was kept at full steam to boil the damp into submission. My brothers and I stayed there in winter when we were small, and to keep warm at night we'd be sent to bed with a hot brick wrapped in an old cloth. It was more efficient than a hot water bottle since it kept its heat for longer, but sleepily unpicking the wrapping with your toes would rouse the household abruptly. My grandparents' outbuildings were full of tins, bottles, boxes, paper and magazines all kept 'just in case they come in handy'. Country-dwellers always have space and no need for the tidiness so beloved of townies.

When it was too wet to wander the fields we'd spend hours ferreting around our grandfather's sheds. Surrounded by paint stripper, two-stroke petrol temptingly decanted into old lemonade bottles, mole traps menacingly hanging from the rafters, old mowers and long-dead vans, the place was more enticing than a theme park and considerably more dangerous. The vast collection of bits of cars, unwanted furniture and assorted junk was rarely called back into service of course, but on the odd occasion that you did need a piece of wood or a headlamp bulb from a Morris 1000, it was good to know it was there (if only you could

find it). Everything had a life and a value beyond its first use – my grandparents had lived through Wales in the 1930s and never tired of telling us to 'waste not', want not'.

They had no fridge – their food was kept in a cave-like stone pantry. They had no washing machine – laundry was all done by hand. The surrounding countryside provided pheasants, beef, salmon, trout, apples and blackberries, so visits to the shops were short and weekly. My grandmother's evenings were often spent darning holed socks and turning worn shirt collars – something I've never seen since. It was a complete anathema to them that you would throw away clothes only part worn.

Later, as teenagers, we'd help take their refuse bag to the end of the lane and marvel that two people could leave so small an impact on the earth compared to our own weekly mountain of rubbish. They lived their lives in simple thrift but now of course they'd be described as 'green'.

Dad, Grampa, me, Gran and Huw

They look tramp-like, their hair matted with constant rain and their own filth covering their hind legs. They're a long way from the 'best in breed' rosettes at the Royal Welsh Show.

The rugged cliff of North Pembrokeshire – the wildest part of the coast path, bearing the full force of the Atlantic.

Fulmars, cormorants, peregrines, kestrels, ravens, wheatears, stonechats and skylarks all thrive on this desolate slab of rock sticking out into the grey sea, though they're keeping their heads down this morning. Even the hardiest bird-watcher might give today a miss and stay at home in the warm.

If it weren't so windy I'd stop for a while, sit on the headland and admire the view towards Dinas Head and my eventual destination, Strumble Head. Behind me I'd ordinarily be able to see Snowdonia, but the mountains are hidden in heavy cloud. Looking at this magnificent, unspoilt view I feel first a sense of great privilege and then – thinking about the distance still to walk – a sense that I should speed up. There's a race to get to Newport, since it looks as though the storm and I have a shared destination.

Hundreds of feet below me, grey seals usually hang out with dolphins and porpoises. I won't see them today, since a successful sighting requires both patience and a viewing position closer to the cliff's edge (and I won't be trying that in this wind). I've sailed around this coast and seen them almost face to face, the seal's whiskers and the dolphin's nose. As I swept past on a borrowed old pilot cutter the dolphins raced alongside us for miles, unable to stop performing.

It's nearly lunchtime and although I haven't been walking that long, I think a short break might be in order – if only to eat some of the weight in my rucksack, which seems to be getting heavier as the hours pass.

Towards Moylgrove

A mile or so beyond Cemaes Head a small derelict brick building sits pointlessly on the edge of the field. Its glassless windows stare out over the sea, which is now uniformly grey save an occasional lick of surf. I think this hut might have been one of the hundreds of wartime coastal lookouts that kept Pembrokeshire's Dad's Army warm while watching for enemy aircraft or submarines. Milford Haven's oil storage tanks were only a short flight from here, and were heavily bombed.

Odd to think that seventy years ago someone else was chewing their sandwiches right here on the North Pembrokeshire coast, listening for strange noises and watching sky and sea. I wonder what they had for lunch. It's a bar of chocolate and a bag of peanuts for me, and a large bottle of water. I could do with a hot drink. It's breezy again now and a nice cup of tea would hit the spot. I bet they had some good brews in this lookout.

DEFENDING THE COAST

For somewhere so far from continental Europe, Pembrokeshire has always been heavily involved in the unpleasant business of war. This coastline is littered with fortifications to defend against foreign invasion, the county's beaches were rehearsal stages for D-Day and later the German army moved to South Pembrokeshire to train after the war. As kids my brothers and I used to stop on the way back from the beach at Freshwater West and scramble over the German tanks Romulus and Remus parked outside Castlemartin range. One of the great contradictions of this National Park is that a huge chunk of it is given over to army training ranges, where the quiet of the countryside is interrupted by tanks blasting targets out at sea. Many a Sunday driver in Pembrokeshire has had the shock of their life after taking a wrong turn and finding themselves facing a tank on manoeuvres, while boatmen who've fallen asleep on a warm day's fishing have been woken by Armageddon.

In the days of black and white my Dad gave a television interview in which he protested about the German army coming to train in Pembrokeshire. He'd served in the Second World War – as had both his brothers – and was deeply critical as were many other Pembrokeshire veterans. There were protests in the streets and you took your life in your hands if you drove a Volkswagen in Pembroke Dock. Dad told the interviewer that not that many years before, the same armed forces who were now making themselves comfortable in his backyard had been sworn enemies, regularly bombing Milford Haven. But in the détente of the new Europe they were now on the same side training in their tanks on the cliffs of Pembrokeshire waiting for the next conflict – the Cold War.

The Germans and their families were greeted with great suspicion. A few German children came to our school and like the well-brought-up worldly types we were we made them feel welcome by reminding them of who won the war.

Decades later the television people came back to interview my Dad to mark the departure of the German troops – they had found his old interview in their archives. Like many others in Pembrokeshire he was saddened to see the Germans leave – they had become pillars of the community who'd enriched the county and had come to love the place.

It's one o'clock and the growing wind causes the long grass to perform a Mexican wave across the field. My ideal walking speed of four miles an hour won't be reached today. I keep stopping and writing and simply being slow. This isn't easy walking either: the uphill stretches are steep and the downhill bits are treacherous mudslides punctuated with unforgiving rocks. This will take much longer than I'd planned – although to be honest I had no real idea of how long this walk would take. The signs on the next gate warn of the dangerous condition of the path and advise the timid to turn back. Stupid really to begin a journey not knowing how long it will take.

Down the cliff now, and I'm closer to foaming sea level. The wooden bridge at Gernos crosses a fast tumbling torrent swollen by rain that has fallen a few miles away on the Preseli Hills. As the path drops I'm able to see the cliffs side-on for the first time. They look brutal, grey and black like the wide folds of skin of a prehistoric animal (the cliffs around most of the south of the county are old red sandstone). At well over 400 feet high, I now understand the earlier warnings. I can see the waves of compression that formed them with unimaginable and explosive force. There's no gentle belly underneath them at their foot, no sandy beach, and no shore to scramble back to safety. Just unforgiving sheer cliff face. This is nature at its most brutal and magnificent.

Geologists call this part of Pembrokeshire the 'northern geological province'. Formed in the Palaeozoic Era, the cliffs here are some 300 million years old (older than those in the south of the county), although some of the oldest rocks may be a thousand million years old. At this point my elementary geology becomes a little hazy.

Back at the top of the cliff, three purple Lycra-clad figures appear on the horizon. They are the first people I've seen in three hours. One of them leads by a good margin of a hundred yards or so; the other two are walking together talking animatedly. I have felt alone all morning but not lonely, and the prospect of making conversation or worse still being joined on my walk suddenly makes me feel uncomfortable. If you spend your time working in teams or in offices there is something almost thrilling about being by yourself on a journey.

It's a man in front and behind two women side by side. The man passes me with a walker's nod (a greeting not unlike a farmer's finger, when a Welsh farmer acknowledges you as he passes on his tractor by raising no more than a finger). It is a small courtesy but sufficient for people who are complete strangers. When the women walkers draw close they stop and chat – they are from Shropshire and down for the weekend. Maybe the man is the boyfriend of one of them – or more likely the husband if he's stalking ahead. Three's a difficult number for walking, particularly on such a narrow path. 'Are you local?' they ask. 'Yes,' I reply. 'You are very lucky,' they say and tell me they have walked from Moylgrove. We exchange goodbyes and they walk on over the path that I've left just behind. They restart their conversation before I'm out of earshot. I'm glad I'm on my own, I know I'd miss drinking in the sights and sounds of the coast if I was concentrating on being good company. This is a selfish endeavour of mine.

The sun is dropping and, cooling, I pull my gloves on for the first time today, my fingers complaining, numb and red with the cold. It's curious what deeper meaning a few words of greeting can contain. Strictly speaking, I've lied to those walkers when I said I was local, but in a sense it does reflect what I truly think. I was born and brought up in Pembrokeshire but I went to school in Mid Wales, then college, a job in London then back 'home' to Wales but to work in Cardiff. Nevertheless, I still like to think I belong here. I live in a city that is convenient for work but I pine to be here when I'm away – yet when I come here I know that I have lived the greater part of my life away from Pembrokeshire. It's odd. That word 'home' is some half-forgotten memory of halcyon days that quite possibly never really existed.

I don't know why I've formed such a strong attachment to this place. Thinking about it, why does anyone form any attachment to a landscape? My parents were fiercely proud of their county and when I was growing up here in the 1970s they were strongly opposed to plans to redraw the electoral map and replace Pembrokeshire with a new entity called Dyfed. A sticker on our car windscreen urged the good people of the county to 'Save Pembrokeshire', as though it were about to be sold off to the Saudi royal family or a Texas oil baron. Life at home witnessed many political discussions about a sense of place. Car drivers started buying the distinctive Pembrokeshire 'DE' number plates in the same way that philatelists collect rare stamps. As a small boy growing up in this community the notion that Pembrokeshire was distinctive and worth fighting for was ingrained – even if, as small children, we never really knew what we were defending or fighting for.

Pembrokeshire is pretty much a microcosm of Wales. The north of the county is farming country and Welsh speaking; the south is industrialized and anglicized. That's a crude characterization but not so far off. Wales is brought together on sporting occasions when we unite to face the old enemies, but otherwise we are a people divided by geography, shopping and language. West Wales looks to Swansea and Cardiff, whereas the real capitals of North Wales are Manchester, Liverpool and Chester. Yet in Pembrokeshire there remains an innate suspicion of Cardiff. In truth we Welsh are not a whole entity but a collection of disparate tribes.

They are more sceptical and distrustful in Pembrokeshire than anywhere else in Wales. This is a constituency that has returned MPs of many different political colours. They are experienced at taking matters into their own hands: for example, when they beat up the French in the last invasion of Britain near Fishguard (during which the French apparently mistook some local women on the hill for soldiers and surrendered), or when the 'Rebecca rioters' (named after the story of Rebekah in Genesis) disguised themselves as women to destroy the much-hated road toll gates that so hampered free trade and travel.

To understand my and Pembrokeshire's identity crisis you have to go back to William the Conqueror and Rhys ap Tewdwr. These lands, known as Deheubarth, were relatively peaceful compared to the rest of the country and Rhys had full control in his neck of the woods. But under William's son, William Rufus, that diplomatic respect and autonomy was revoked and in an advance from Shrewsbury to the coast at Pembroke, Welsh was ethnically cleansed from what we now call Pembrokeshire – the language's memorial is the string of terrifying castles lacing the landscape.

There's suddenly an overpowering smell of farmyard manure – not a quick waft but industrial amounts that seem to resist even the strengthening wind. These days the little farms that once characterized west Wales have pretty much gone – only huge acreages can turn profits or attract subsidies. You'll find a few hobby farmers and smallholders here and there, but selling off the farmhouse to some nice middle-class family and then fusing together various separate holdings is often the only economically viable option for agriculture around here. Passing foul-smelling farms, my father used to antagonize my mother – who always wanted to return to live in the country – by opening the car window further, take theatrical deep breaths pretending to enjoy what he called 'the smell of the country'. My mother would quickly explain to her three small children the odour came from silage, before my father offered another word for the agricultural whiff. He was an unreconstructed townie, my mother always a country girl – and I take after them both.

CHILDHOOD IN PEMBROKESHIRE

rowing up in South Pembrokeshire in the 1970s was like living in the Home Counties. The schools taught in English, and the Welsh language was given the same amount of time as woodwork. The curriculum made little mention of the historic struggle of the Welsh. It was much the same in Monmouthshire, Newport and Cardiff, and many other anglicized areas of Wales.

At home our television aerial, like thousands of others, was aimed towards the West Country transmitter so my parents could avoid receiving Welsh language television (which replaced some of their favourite BBC programmes). The rise of cottage-burning Welsh nationalists troubled my law-abiding parents, who felt alienated by any sort of nationalism, Welsh or otherwise. In English-speaking South Pembrokeshire they didn't feel comfortable with the rise of a movement that seemed to set itself against people like us. The vandalism of road signs and occupation of council offices sent a shiver down their backs. We thought of ourselves as Welsh, and our

families on both sides were of ancient Pembrokeshire stock, but the rise of the Welsh nationalist movement would find no sympathy in Pembroke Dock. My parents were quite happy not to have their gas bill printed in Welsh. There in that microcosm of our family, you encapsulate the unease of contemporary Wales. Most of the country doesn't speak Welsh, yet many of those people would regard themselves as Welsh.

The historical injustices of strangling the language, religious persecution and political under-representation are now slowly being reversed. We have a new (and yet to be loved) Welsh Assembly, though its establishment by the narrowest of electoral margins divided the country. The two devolution votes were symptomatic of a people weary of distant faceless Westminster power and yet cautious of a new political authority closer to home. The country that once sat enraptured listening to poets and preachers, and that gave Britain some of its most stirring politicians, is sceptical even of its own newfound power.

Who needs toys? Me and my brother Huw on the beach at Freshwater East in South Pembrokeshire

21

 *Ceibwr Bay*

My hamstrings are beginning to twang and give notice of some serious limping tomorrow. The cliffs of Ceibwr Bay are jet black and full of the most magnificent swirls, textbook examples of geological faulting and folding, wonderfully contorted by the earth's movements 450 million years ago. At 575 feet these are some of the highest points on the coast path. A slate and stone footbridge carries me over the stream, its water level swollen and racing for the sea. Coming into view on the far bank an old cream-coloured tractor is parked at the side of the track with a fishing boat on its trailer. On closer inspection, they both seem welded to the spot – the tyres are soft and there's a sweet smell of old engine oil from a leaking tank. Their wheels couldn't have moved this summer.

Once this was the port serving the little community of Moylgrove just up the valley, in a time when, before roads and railways, all of Pembrokeshire's goods arrived and departed by water. The

The cliffs at Ceibwr Bay rise to a height of 575 feet, one of the highest points on the coast path.

grey sea has been pretty much empty of ships today but once it would have carried all manner of goods and people around the coast and across the world. Flat-bottomed boats would beach on the shale here, to unload their cargoes of limestone. This would have been transferred to carts to be taken to the kilns – after being burnt it would have been spread over the fields to improve the land. Like so many of Pembrokeshire's little harbours, the fate of Ceibwr Bay was sealed by the coming of the railways and the motor car. Great crowds came to watch the last little ship berth here in 1926.

Wynford Vaughan-Thomas's ghost looms large here, too: he once owned this land and gave it to the National Trust in 1983. I feel a small burst of pride every time I pass one of their signs, since it's the only organization I belong to. I never gave a moment's thought to safeguarding the landscape until I was in my late thirties. Maybe you don't really appreciate the importance of the countryside until you are older. But the more I think about my life growing up here, the more aware I become of how much I owe to a childhood spent roaming free in the countryside. Now I'd like everyone to be able to enjoy what I did.

 Moylgrove

The clouds are gathering rather ominously. I decide to have a five-minute breather sitting on the stone bridge, to watch the water and eat the last of my food. I know that I have not made the distance that I should have, and I'm going to be late to my destination in Newport – which means the last stage will be in the dark, on a muddy path, clinging to the cliff top. None of which is ideal. My legs are still aching and in an exceptional piece of bad planning I've forgotten to wear my heavy-duty socks – when I take off my boots to give my feet a rub my toes are raw and my soles badly blistered. But the landscape and the sheer joy of being here are too seductive to quit. I feel a sense of release and achievement to have got this far, so I'm going to keep going to Newport, some three hours' walk away. Not that I have much choice, of course: there's no mobile phone reception and the tourist buses won't be driving by until next summer.

When I decide to get going again I have to move onto my hands and knees first to stand – my hamstrings are stiffening up. Happily there is no one around to see me on all fours. Here there are no cars and no noise, save for the waves slumping lethargically on the shore. Moylgrove wasn't always such a quiet and peaceful place – in the nineteenth century there were nine pubs in this tiny village. And in the seventeenth century William, the only son of Thomas Perkins of Trefaes (just up the road), was hanged for murder. The guidebooks don't go into the details of his crime, but it might be wise not to loiter for too long.

Pwll y Wrach

After a mile or so, I come across another great excuse to stop and stare. Dug deep out of the headland behind the coast path is a quarry-like hole, fringed on its top by a ginger bracken quiff. This is Pwll y Wrach – the Witch's Cauldron – and is in fact a collapsed cave where the waves have undermined the cliff, battering the rock into submission. The action of the tide ripping in and out makes the most wonderful sucking noises. Just to the south of Pwll y Wrach the Iron Age hill fort of Castell Treriffith was given to the National Trust by Wynford Vaughan-Thomas. On a kinder day I would clamber up and take some pictures. Rather implausibly this sleepy little bay was the centre of an international drug smuggling operation in the 1980s.

It's now half past four and a cold dusk signals its arrival by showing my breath. I'd like to be able to tell you that the last seven miles of this journey are all being meticulously recorded in my red-and-black lined notebook, but that would be a lie. This morning's notes are frequent, voluminous and easy to read, but as the hours pass they are becoming shorter, more illegible and blurred by raindrops. The bottom third of the book is dripping wet, too. I like to think I have prepared for the worst that late autumn can throw at me. I have perfect boots for long-distance walking: they are well broken in and comfortable. My waterproof jacket and trousers are standing up well to November and so too is my thermal hat so beloved of mountaineering friends (who always remind me of the importance of keeping your head warm).

However, apart from my socks, I also overlooked the need for a good waterproof rucksack. My ancient model has done a splendid job of soaking up all the rain and then pooling it inside so that my notebook has absorbed the water, making my hieroglyphics increasingly unreadable – even to me. Not that it matters much any more, since even wearing gloves my hands are too cold to hold a pen and it's getting too dark to write…as I neglected to bring a torch.

I had thought nightfall would be another half an hour away but heavy clouds have brought the dark forwards. Nevertheless I still feel a huge sense of adventure just being here in such dramatic countryside. I'm not a typical Welshman in that I love the sun (which makes rare appearances in this country), but wrapped up warm, the breathtaking cliff-top landscape really is something to behold. I'm going to pretend that I haven't seen the speed with which the black clouds are racing across the Irish Sea – they look like a dog that has caught sight of you on the horizon and is bounding over menacingly.

Lundy and Irish Sea: Gales Now Rising

It looks like the weather forecaster was right after all. The onslaught begins with large drops of rain – the introit to a screaming gale that I'd hoped would find another victim. I had planned on being long finished and indoors by the time the gale force winds and torrential rain struck Pembrokeshire. There is nothing particularly dangerous about walking in a gale – in fact, there is something invigorating about feeling so in touch with the elements, particularly if you're togged up snugly – but walking along a cliff top in the growing darkness is something I had not prepared myself for. The only consolation comes after a gust of wind nearly blows me off my feet and I realize that if I am going to be blown over, the wind will dump me in the hedge to my left rather than the sea to my right. Small comfort, but comfort still.

Over the fields in the shapeless black is the farm at Trefwrdan Uchaf and in the far distance the huddle of houses that is Gethsemane. But they are hidden in the valley that falls away from the headland; no lights shine from their milking parlours or barns. They are there, though, somewhere.

All my life I have tried to stay out of storms (I happily admit that I skived off games when it was raining), but here there is nowhere to shelter. Besides, sheltering will only delay my arrival and the wind and rain show no sign of letting up – the storm could go on all night. I can feel the water run down my neck, not just a few drips but cupfuls of cold. My legs are beginning to resemble those of the ponies I saw earlier, the backs of my waterproof trousers covered in mud from falling and slipping. Head bowed, leaning into the wind, eyes on the path, I am flailing around. The wind catches the loose material around my hood and slaps me round my face. I have walked not much more than two miles in the last hour. You can't really get lost on the coast path in the way that mountaineers get lost on Snowdon – after all, there's only one direction to go – but you can get disorientated. The wind is now so strong that I don't dare stop to open my map, since it would just get blown away.

The headland in front of me gives some twenty minutes of shelter and relief from the force of the wind, although not the rain, but as soon as I climb back up the hill the Atlantic greets me head on and scowling. When I was a kid we were taken to see *King Lear* at the Royal Shakespeare Company in Stratford and we marvelled at the way the special effects people created howling gales and pouring rain in the middle of a theatre. Lear, naked and soaked, windblown and desolate, raged against the screaming of the storm. Funny what goes through your mind when you know you must keep your spirits up.

Pembrokeshire's storm this evening is theatrical, too. Even my waterproofs are now pretty much pointless; I might as well be naked for all the protection they provide. I can't see much in front of me, either. It's only in deep countryside like this, miles from the nearest street light, that you really experience complete darkness. My eyes are swimming with rainwater driving straight into my face, and I can feel my contact lenses slipping around. I always get nervous swimming underwater in case I lose my lenses, but the possibility of losing them while walking is a new experience.

As I mentioned earlier, the coast path varies in quality from recently built sections of gravelled hard standing – complete with wooden bridges and stiles lovingly built by volunteers last summer – to a rock slide of mud not much better than a medieval track. I, for one, prefer it this way, even in these horrid conditions. Nothing would be worse than this spectacular landscape becoming home to an easy gravelled path – the wild landscape should be accompanied by a path that is an adventure, an ordeal even.

I've fallen over four times now; it's a mark of the fear of falling and breaking a bone in the dark that you find yourself gripping onto rusty barbed wire fences for security, but even the barbs and the warm stickiness on my hands is preferable to spending the night out here with a broken ankle.

I am squatting on the downhill sections of the path, reasoning that if I do slip on the soaked and polished protruding rocks I will not fall so far. My grandparents used to walk like this in their declining years – small shuffles in a short gait to be certain of staying upright. The rain has made the next section almost too slippery to walk on, and one hill I can only climb on my hands and knees, snatching onto the grass verge and hedge; a gorse bush hidden in the darkness bites my hand and makes me cry out.

I need a break for just a moment, and there's a high Pembrokeshire earth hedge to shelter against. It no longer matters that the grassy earth that I'm leaning against is soaking my clothes, since they are already sodden. I look back over my route, but the blackened cliffs, headlands and fields have all disappeared into darkness and the rain has covered my tracks.

I've always taken notice of news stories about climbers who come to grief – it's usually the result of getting tired, getting lost, getting cold or breaking something. There are no more walkers on the path now – no one starts out in darkness and no one starts out in conditions like this. I don't feel rested one bit after that breather but know that I must carry on and occupy myself with positive thoughts. I must keep my mind busy with anything. So I try to remember the words to the song 'Delilah' – not as frivolous an exercise as it sounds, since I'm going to be singing this very song with my newsroom colleagues next week on television as part of the BBC's Children in Need appeal. However, I find that I can't even remember an entire line. This isn't helping.

I fail to find my foothold and go flying again; I land flat on my back, the combination of stones and mud on the path pummel my backside like a massage from a sadist. This is ritual humiliation; I am undergoing an ordering from the natural world and I have been firmly put in my place. There's nothing broken, but my hands are cut and bruised and I will scare small children when eventually I emerge muddy and bloody at the other end. I can't remember when I last got injured, fell over or was cut as badly as this – in school rugby perhaps, or falling off my bike as a child.

I can feel myself losing concentration and I'm getting cold and tired. My mind is flailing around, the gearbox never quite engaging with any one thought. I think of slipping gently but awkwardly into a hot bath late tonight; the Aston Martin in the new Bond film, a pint of bitter (though not in that order perhaps).

In the far distance in the black waves I can just pick out the faint white sweep of a beam from Strumble Head lighthouse. My heart leaps for a moment until I remember that if this is Strumble Head lighthouse then I still have a long way to walk. Those sweeps of light emanate from miles away; in total darkness any light is deceptive. It's still too windy to open out the map, and I'd be pushed to say exactly where I am, apart from between Moylgrove and Newport. I can no longer see the path and gingerly feel my way along where I think it should be. The barbed wire fence to my left is my constant (if unlikely) friend.

Somewhere beyond the fence and the seemingly endless darkness of the fields beside me must be the high ground of Foel Goch or perhaps its smaller brother Foel Fach – and between them, in the distance, the little hamlet of Gethsemane. So why can't I see any lights? I know that there are farms somewhere near here. Someone somewhere must be watching television, making tea or in the bathroom and they must need to switch on a light. Half-deafened in my soaking hood, the only sounds I can hear are the endless wind and the hard splatter of driving rain.

 *Newport in Sight*

Suddenly, around the next turn in the path inland and away from the sea, I can see the lights of Newport. In a car it would take no time at all but for me it's still a good half-hour's shuffle. I'm nearing the end of an initiation – I feel a curious sense of relief to see the ordinariness of street lamps and chimneys. I feel elation too that I have not given up or been beaten. Still far away I can see a bus, its lights on in search of passengers to fill its empty seats. Who'd be mad enough to want to go anywhere on a night like this? I feel a huge sense of pride and achievement too; and a tiny tinge of regret that my tryst with dark nature is over and I'm stepping back into the light. My face is on fire from burning wind and rain – I've never felt so alive. Now I just need to find the cottage where I'm staying tonight....

Chapter Two

The Pembrokeshire Coast Path *(Part II)*

NEVERN ● PRESELI HILLS ● NEWPORT ●

CAT ROCK AND CWM YR EGLWYS ● DINAS ISLAND ●

FISHGUARD ● GOODWICK ● STRUMBLE HEAD

*I*N THE first moments of waking I become aware that I am not in my usual surroundings and that I have some unusual aches in unfamiliar places. This is not my usual bed or my usual bedroom, and then I remember where I am and what I was doing the previous day. I have rented an old cottage lying in the middle of a triangle made up of Felindre Farchog, Moylgrove and Nevern, just outside Newport. It's surrounded by moorland and is as secluded as it's possible to be on these crowded islands. There's no mobile phone reception, no telephone landline and no internet access. The cottage is typical of Pembrokeshire – squat and foursquare, with a distinctly home-made look. The render outside and the plaster inside have been applied by hand, and there are finger marks where the wet slurry has been pushed between proud stones and into deep corners. It's the perfect place to stay for a couple of nights – anything more luxurious would jar with my austere pilgrimage.

The iconic lighthouse at Strumble Head, marking my journey's end.

There is magic in this part of North Pembrokeshire, something supernatural about these dark forests and unchanging gentle hills where the winter mist rarely lifts. The beguiling mix of fable and history is intoxicating. I used to come here with my grandfather in his Morris Minor when I was learning to drive. You'd never pass another car, and we'd get lost in unmarked lanes. He never seemed to mind, though – we had all the time in the world and he shared my love of pottering around.

 *Nevern*

Though I'm keen to get back to the coast path, I know that my blisters need a day off – and besides, there's a wealth of things to see just on my doorstep. So today I decide to head inland to explore the delights of Nevern – which mostly revolve around its fascinating church and castle. Along the back lanes it's no more than an hour's walk away.

The church at Nevern sits in a steep wooded valley, in shadow for much of the day. A narrow stone bridge and a shabby, unloved vicarage share the same view of the distant mountain. It couldn't be more perfect. Though the church is ancient, it's cheering to see that it's still in weekly use. There has been a chapel on this site since as early as 540, making it one of the older places of worship in Wales. I used to laugh at my father's insistence on stopping to explore every church and graveyard that we passed, but now I find myself doing the same; I wish he was still around to enjoy our shared passion.

We called in here once on a school trip and, as children do, sniggered at the frequent mentions of Nevern's bleeding yew and the mounting block by the graveyard. One of the twisted old trees has dark red resin dripping from an old wound in the trunk and it does indeed look like blood. One of the many legends surrounding its history is that a monk was hanged from its branches for a crime he didn't commit. In his dying moments he cried that the tree would bleed forever to proclaim his innocence.

The church is dedicated to St Brynach, an Irishman (though some think he was native Welsh) who may have lived in a retreat above Newport on Carn Ingli – the Hill of the Angels. According to legend, Brynach was the victim of a vicious spear attack by a woman whose advances he'd rejected in Llanfrynach. (Note to self – never reject the advances of a woman in Llanfrynach, particularly if carrying spear.) The holy man survived to tell the tale and eventually moved on to this quieter parish where he introduced new farming techniques. King Clether was so impressed by Brynach's labours that he gave him his lands and retired to Cornwall as a Christian hermit (even then people were retiring to Cornwall). It's said that you'll hear the first cuckoo in Wales in Nevern churchyard on Brynach's feast day, 7 April.

Huw, me and Richard in Pembroke Dock Cemetery on one of Dad's instructive trips.

UNRAVELLING THE RUNES

*I*t's the ancient carved stones that entice historians to Nevern church. Inside, in the south transept, the Maglocunus Stone, carved in Latin and Ogham lettering, commemorates Maglocunus, son of Clutor, and is thought to date from the fifth century. The Cross Stone beside it has an intricate Celtic interlace pattern. In the churchyard, the Vitalianus Stone and the Great Cross – standing some 13 feet high – is one of the best Celtic crosses in the country. There is something truly humbling about standing next to such intricate work, chiselled to perfection so many centuries ago.

In the 1840s the vicar of the parish, the Reverend John Jones, and Lady Charlotte Guest copied the Mabinogion – a collection of Celtic myths – into English. Many of the stories contained in the Mabinogion come from the nearby Preseli Hills – the legends about love and valour from the Dark Ages had been passed on by word of mouth and written down in medieval times. A memorial to the Reverend Jones stands beside the old yews. Here, on the pilgrimage route to St David's, is Wales at its most ancient and beautiful. If history can speak to us, then this churchyard is perhaps the best place to listen.

Having seen the church, I now head over to the castle, which, unlikely as it sounds, has been making the headlines recently. Archaeologists from Durham University have been excavating the site in an attempt to piece together its history. This was originally a native Welsh stronghold but was seized in the twelfth century by the Norman Robert Fitzmartin, Lord of Cemaes. Later in that century, determined to bring an end to years of feuding, the Welshman Lord Rhys promised peace with the Fitzmartins with the marriage of his daughter Angharad to the Fitzmartins' son William. But, as is often the case when dealing with prospective in-laws, there was soon trouble and in 1191 Lord Rhys stormed Nevern and handed it over to his sons. The Fitzmartins moved down the road to Newport and built a grander castle and Lord Rhys ended up a prisoner in Nevern Castle, kept there by his own sons. This of course provided endless amusement to my brothers and me when we were young.

There isn't much left of the castle now – this isn't one of those Welsh strongholds like Pembroke or Caernarfon that has hordes of tourists trouping over the battlements. However, the original motte (a small artificial hill favoured by the Normans) can still be seen among the overgrown ruins. The archaeologists' scrapings this summer will recover some of the ancient history of Wales concealed for centuries beneath the damp earth.

 *Preseli Hills*

Having seen just about everything that Nevern has to offer, and being wary of pushing myself too hard today, I've decided to head back to the cottage. After miles of high hedges obscuring my view suddenly there's a gap allowing a breathtaking view of Dinas Island in the distance; Carn Ingli rises above to the clouds and the coastline's long arm stretches for miles beyond. From the top of the track to the cottage you can see the sea – at least if it's one of those clear crisp winter days. There's no sea view from the cottage, which is nestled in a dip. As I turn into the track by the old milk churn stand, the Preseli Hills form the backdrop to what must rank as one of the most achingly beautiful locations in Britain. Every time I stop and look my heart misses a beat.

We have a soft spot for the Preselis in our family. When we were kids growing up on the other side of the county we'd come here for a picnic often with grandparents in tow and after boiled eggs and damp sandwiches on a tartan rug we'd spend the afternoon running wild in these hills as only three small boys can. For children fond of shouting, screaming and toy guns, the bleakness and isolation was a welcome haunt. Even then, we realized this was a different kind of Pembrokeshire from the one we knew at home.

The Preseli Hills are the last gasp of the Cambrian Mountains, the range that pops up here and there the length of Wales. Near the coast they are a delight of open moorland, hills and forests rising to 1760 feet – which may not sound high compared with Snowdon or Ben Nevis, but here we are proud of them, even if we can't decide whether to call them the Preseli Hills or Mountains. From the summit of Foel Cwmcerwyn on a clear day you can see Ireland's Wicklow Mountains to the west and sometimes the Snowdonia range to the north. On a misty day you'll be unnerved by their silence and standing stones and be transported back to an ancient Britain. On the far side of the Preselis, towards the border with Carmarthenshire, the hills' majesty has been somewhat besmirched by two television masts and a wind farm. But they are the only distractions from a landscape groaning with treasures. Among the millions of dirty sheep and hundreds of mountain ponies the hills are covered with the remains of prehistoric man; cairns, burial chambers, standing stones and circles all built before Christianity came to these shores. From the summits you can see the Neolithic dolmen of Pentre Ifan, the remains of an Iron Age fort and a little further away the reconstructed huts at the Romano-British fort at Castell Henllys.

The Preselis were the stronghold of Arthurian legend and Celtic culture, and its foothills the entrance to Annwn, the underworld. The beaches, the coastline and the mountains are an intrinsic part of childhood if you grow up in Pembrokeshire – here the Preseli Hills transcend ownership and boundaries; they are everyone's playground.

Few quiet Augusts pass in Wales without another stoking of the debate of how Stonehenge got its Preseli Bluestones. Did the ancients really transport them all the way from Pembrokeshire to Wiltshire, or was it ice that dumped them so conveniently at the feet of the builders? In 2000, an experiment sought to end the discussion once and for all by dragging a boulder from the Preselis on rollers and strapping it between two large coracles. Unfortunately after a promising start to the journey, filmed by the country's media, the great stone sank without trace, which goes to show if nothing else that our ancestors could balance a boat more competently than we can.

I tear myself away from the view and walk onto the track that leads eventually to the cottage. I didn't really pay attention to my surroundings last night – mostly because I arrived in total darkness. The track to the cottage meanders downhill for a mile, winding gently over potholes swimming with circles of rain. On either side of the ruts, the open fields and a copse of gnarled trees are the hiding places of fox and pheasant. The industrialized fields and their harshly cut hedges back on the main road give way here to softer unkempt boundaries. The trees are modest and grow short and stunted – like figures frozen in a parlour game, their boughs and branches are distorted and deformed by the wind that blows from one direction. Halfway down the track a ruined cottage has been almost returned to the earth, claimed by ivy and saplings.

BATTLE FOR THE PRESELIS

*U*nlike parts of Castlemartin and the Brecon Beacons (which are home to military ranges), the Preselis are fully open to the public. Saving the Preseli Hills for the nation is an episode of recent Welsh history that has almost been lost. Were it not for this community rising up to defy the might of the War Office under Clement Attlee's post-Second World War government, the hills would be ringed with barbed wire and shot to pieces in target practice. The War Office intended to evict more than 200 farmers from their homes in 1947 and transform the Preseli Hills into a permanent military training ground.

But within a few weeks of the announcement, the Precelly (sic) Preservation Committee was formed under the guidance of Nonconformist ministers, village schoolmasters and other public figures. A meeting was held at Brynberian when one minister after another rose to their feet to underline the 'sanctity' of the hills – after all, even in prehistory locals were building monuments on the slopes, while the bluestones that form Stonehenge on Salisbury Plain were taken from here. Surely no Englishman would defile an area to which he had such strong historical connections?

By the spring of 1948 the battle had been won. It was a story of success in safeguarding a community compared to what was sadly lost on Mynydd Epynt in Mid Wales a few years earlier, where families made way for military training. Yet other battles remained to be fought, and years after this episode, far north from here at Tryweryn, near Bala, families watched in disbelief and despair as their chapel, graveyard, houses and gardens disappeared under the water of the new reservoir built to provide water for England.

Across the fields from here I can just about make out Bayvil's tiny church, standing alone in the trees. St Andrew's is thought to be an early nineteenth-century rebuilding of a medieval church, its single chamber interior, almost cell-like in its simplicity. Inside is a twelfth-century square font and an elaborate memorial tablet to Morris Williams of Cwmgloyne, who died in 1840, which seems almost out of place in such modest surroundings.

Over the cattle grid, and past the huge cold pond (its little rowing boat pulled onto the bank for winter), and finally, through the trees and hedges, the cottage comes into view. Its ancient stone walls are battered and flecked by years of sunshine and storms, alternately freezing and baking its paint. This is not the construction of builders or craftsmen with their precise lines and chiselled masonry but of farm workers on their days off lending an inexpert hand.

There are no keys to unlock the doors or windows, just a wooden finger catch to fasten the entrance door, which opens onto a large flagstoned room. In one corner is the kitchen, full of odd bits of crockery; in another the Aga, belting out heat and offering the promise of food. There is also a scrub-topped table and chairs waiting for dinner and beyond that a Welsh dresser heaving with chipped blue and white china. The door to the small pantry opens inwards onto walls lined with slate shelves – its single wooden shutter fails hopelessly to keep out November's freeze.

The hearth is a simple opening in the wall. Three venerable patched leather armchairs huddle around it – they have eavesdropped on generations of nightcaps by firelight. Alongside them, an old brown wooden bureau has been perfectly positioned to distract any writer with the views onto the garden.

My rented Pembrokeshire cottage, complete with ancient wooden beams, a desk to write at and stunning views to distract me.

An unsteady spiral staircase leads the way upstairs, where an outsize stone fireplace dominates the wide floorboards in what is now the only bedroom. A haughty carved chair looks a little out of place; at one time it must have belonged to grander surroundings than these, perhaps a castle or a church. The simple, undecorated four-poster bed sits in a vast space, its white cotton sheets disappearing into the rough white lime-washed walls.

When this was still a working farmhouse, these two open spaces, upstairs and down, would have been partitioned off into four or perhaps even six tiny, box-like rooms. Before the current age of privacy, the farmer and his family would have all lived here in close proximity and shared the sounds, sights and smells that we now hide. The small square windows of grey oak and whitewashed walls imbue an atmosphere of almost monastic simplicity. Chapels and churches often emanate a sense of healing by virtue of their years, and this place has a similar feel. There is nothing new here, everything is generations old and well used. It's a building with human scale – the wooden rafters of the bedroom floor are in easy touching distance above my head. The walls look as though they grew from the rock not far beneath the earth, and the irregular wood beams, uneven slate floors, window sills and flag stones hide nothing of their origins.

I make a fire from ash logs placed on a bed of dry twigs – hopefully this will burn all night. What is it about staying for a few nights in a rented house that brings such contentedness? It must be the unaccustomed physical exhaustion of the 15 miles I covered yesterday; or perhaps the fresh air of winter and being alone in the elements.

My leg muscles are stiffening by the hour and most parts of me are aching. There is no shower here; instead there is a slipper bath in a lean-to at the side of the cottage. Lying in the foam, I watch my big toe nail turn purple before black, the only casualty of yesterday's hike.

Despite my exhaustion and the crisp linen sheets, I cannot sleep for some time. The sounds of the countryside on the prowl keep me awake. This is the chorus of the rural night-time, a sometimes uneasy accompaniment for a townie used to different nocturnal sounds. The footfall of a dog or a fox close by makes my heart race. Later, after a few hours' fitful sleep, a vixen's bark wakes me with a start in the small hours. I am a long way from anywhere and for a fleeting moment that realisation alarms me. Now, wide awake and heart beating fast, I can smell the wood smoke from the still burning fire below and wonder whether to go downstairs and sit by the embers to read and simply enjoy being here.

Back on the Coast Path

It's a treacherously cold but bright and sunny morning in the way winter days in Wales can surprise and delight you. As a Welshman, one expects to be rained on for much of the year, so when the day is dry we are doubly blessed. (Of course, when the day is wet we take an immodest pride in the fulfilment of our predictions.)

Waking in the countryside is different to being roused in the town. Here there is no human noise. There is birdsong, of course, and much of it loud and raucous; but there are no neighbours sleepily setting off car alarms as they leave for work, no street cleaners, no newspaper or postal delivery. Here they leave their bundle in an old bread bin at the end of the lane.

The cottage's Aga has been kind and warmed the cold stone. Sunlight strides past the edges of the unfurled straw beach mats that stand in as window blinds. The air still hangs heavy with last night's ash logs. Christmas has come a month early to Pembrokeshire; the heaviest frost of winter has fallen on the fields below the Preselis and nothing moves – save for the Welsh ponies in the neighbouring field grazing unperturbed by their white pasture. The hard surface of the pond confuses the birds landing for breakfast. The last time the sky was this blue it was summer, but it is also bitterly cold.

My muscles have been thoroughly twanged by the exertions of the past couple of days. This morning the usually unconscious actions of pulling on a shirt and trousers seem to make me feel like an old man dressing – every movement is slow and deliberate. I'm aching all over despite a reasonable night's sleep and am probably not in the best shape for another long day's walk from Newport to Lower Fishguard.

Outdoors, the air is hard and visible and almost uncomfortable to breath. In bright daylight, the coast path that seemed so harsh and cruel a couple of nights ago is almost welcoming. The other evening in pouring rain I left the path beside Newport's empty golf course above the town. This morning in dazzling sunlight it's teeming with players. I'm no golfer but, if I were I can't imagine a more spectacular place to spend the day, even if the sudden Atlantic gusts must make for a challenging round. I nearly came to grief clinging onto the coast path the other night, but this morning, picking up the path again and crossing the golf course, dodging the balls is just as dangerous.

 *Newport*

Newport was once the capital of the Marcher lordship of Cemaes. The castle built in the thirteenth century frowns over the church and graveyard and towers above the narrow little streets that struggle with cars and lorries. The newer part of town is the expensive sprawl alongside the golf course; here, away from the shadow of the hill, the afternoon sun lingers longer and the view towards the sea is unbroken. But these newer houses couldn't look more out of keeping with the rest of the town's beautiful stone houses. For a county so blessed with such a wealth of built heritage, Pembrokeshire's planners sometimes have an extraordinary lack of empathy for their surroundings. (Not so far from here you'll find ugly bungalows obscuring Roch's ancient castle and a huge 1960s tower block ruining the skyline of Tenby's picturesque harbour.)

The Neolithic burial chamber marker known as Carreg Coetan, just outside Newport.

I imagine that it was just above the estuary at the best crossing point with a view across the bay that William Fitzmartin hurriedly built his first wooden stronghold after he was ousted from Nevern. In the field above the coast path there is a crescent-shaped earthwork known as Hen Gastell. It looks across to the town and the present-day stone castle. Behind Hen Gastell is Berry Hill Farm, its farmhouse hiding an earlier wing overlooking the land granted to the Knights Hospitallers of St John between 1198 and 1230.

After diligently following the sea for so many miles since St Dogmaels, at Newport the coast path sweeps inland for a bit to cross the bridge over the Nevern Estuary. This morning the tide is low, and beyond the old limekiln, halfway across the old iron bridge, a sign on a gate warns gunmen not to shoot at birds. Just by the crossing I see another Neolithic dolmen, again marking a burial chamber, known as Carreg Coetan. Though not quite as impressive or as large as that at Pentre Ifan, it's still a remarkable thing, just about big enough to crouch under.

Since I'm doing OK for time, I'm going to leave the coast path for an hour or so and divert into the centre of Newport for a bit of exploring. It's still early in the morning, and a few weekenders are wandering around the gift shops and restaurant windows gazing at menus posted for later bookings; outside the Spar a farmer has left his tractor in the middle of the road while he collects his newspapers. It's a sensible choice of vehicle on a morning when many of the back roads will be impassable with black ice. The butcher hangs a brace of pheasant from his striped shop awning; they are still in feather and look exotic.

The best view of Newport is from the graveyard of St Mary's Church, built in the thirteenth century by William Fitzmartin, the grandson of the first invader of Cemaes. All that remains of the original Norman building is the tower and the font – the church was extensively rebuilt in 1879. The twin powers of Church and State kept a watchful eye over the bay. Through the iron gate, the back of the graveyard is wonderfully wild, its fragile graves scruffy and settling unevenly with time, its tombstones tilting awkwardly to peer over waving long grass. There's nothing remarkable about the church. It has few of the artefacts of Nevern, and none of the grandeur of St David's Cathedral or the piety of Pontfaen in the Gwaun Valley a few miles behind the hills.

Here, there was no landed gentry to cram it with monuments. The gravestones outside and memorials within commemorate the lives of fishermen, sailors, farmers and their families who were once the life and soul of the town.

The church is unlocked, which is something of a surprise these days but perhaps not so uncommon in these parts. The black ring needs a shove to swing open the thick weathered door, and straight away I'm overwhelmed by the smell of candles and wax polish. It's not much warmer inside than out, the winter sun having yet to do its magic and colour the stained glass into a rainbow of light. The organ console beside the choir stalls is unlocked. Sitting on the bench and switching on the bellows I ruin *In the Bleak Mid Winter* on the swell keyboard and then try the pedals too before stopping with regret that I no longer remember much from my childhood playing.

I pass back through the churchyard gate, and Newport Castle sits haughtily over the streets and passages below. Three castles have stood on this site: the first was destroyed by Llywelyn the Great in 1215; the second was destroyed by Llywelyn ap Gruffydd in 1257; and the third was destroyed by Owain Glyndwr between 1400 and 1409. Just think what that did for Pembrokeshire's household insurance premiums.

The ruin that remains looks just the way a castle ought to – terrifying and haunted, yet at the same time decrepit. There is none of your usual sandblasted stone, no metal guide rails, warning signs or life-resuscitation equipment. This is simply an ancient castle that looks as though it might fall down at any time – and is all the more charming for it. Ivy creeps out of the walls, chasing away mortar. PRIVATE PROPERTY signs hang where ordinarily ENTRANCE and CAR PARK would be. A more recent mansion has been built in the remains of the old gatehouse, but it's been a good while since its black-and-white windows saw a coat of paint. Standing at the unwelcoming entrance I wonder what lies within – whatever secrets it holds they could never be as interesting or exciting as I imagine them to be.

At different times this has been the family seat of the Martins, the Audleys, the Tuckets, the Owens (sadly no relation) and the Lloyds. This part of North Pembrokeshire became a Norman March to be defended against the Welsh. After Llywelyn the Great seized the castle in 1215 it was soon returned to the Martins, who passed the title on to a nephew, the 2nd Lord Audley. Audley's descendant James was beheaded in the reign of Henry VI and the Crown took possession of the castle. Eventually the castle was restored to Audley's son, who then sold it in 1543 to the Owens of Henllys. The lawyer George Owen wanted the title rather than the castle – still with me?

Just when you thought it was impossible to squeeze any more drama out of a pile of stones not much larger than Albert Square, the Owen family faced a 19-year legal battle to recover the Barony of Cemaes and George Owen's unfortunate imprisonment in his own dungeon. George Owen was a renowned author, and a copy of his *Description of Penbrockshire* is sitting on my mantelpiece at home, alongside a Jeffrey Archer novel. (Interesting trivia question: name five British authors who've been in prison).

The estate is advertising for tenants to live in Newport Castle, on a lease of twenty or so years. The prospective occupiers have modest quarters to inhabit, but the privilege of living in a piece of living history. (Admittedly the gas bills may be on the steep side.)

Even today there is something splendidly feudal about Newport; the present Lady Marcher continues to exercise the privilege of nominating the town's mayor. This is one of those places I instantly feel at home in. For me, the setting of the castle, church and the rows of houses on the

The Castle Hotel, Bridge Street, Newport, clad in the wonderfully coloured local stone.

OVERLEAF: *Morning at Newport Beach, with some rather ominous grey clouds overhead.*

edge of the mountain staring over the sea place it among the loveliest towns in Wales. Its houses and public buildings are understated and short on pomp, while its narrow lanes are enticing. It's also caught in something of a time warp – come here in the summer and Newport is full of families walking to the beach with their windbreaks; it's like Britain in the 1950s.

Newport is quiet now the hustle and bustle of the summer's visitors has passed. The old town is built in the shadow of the mountain, meaning that winter evenings come early. In July and August the place is stuffed with visitors renting or staying in their cottages. Some here will breathe a sigh of relief now that their favourite perch in the café is theirs again and the tourists' 4x4s no longer double-park on the pavements; but those dependent on the visitors' pounds know it's a long time until they return next Easter. Many of these small stone houses are holiday homes – like so much of coastal Wales, the locals can't afford to live here any more. In high season, the town is wealthy and buzzing, its restaurants fully booked and shops crowded. But in winter Newport shows a sadder side – its bookshop closed for good this year, the restaurants and cafés open for only a few evenings a week and the permanent residents seem mostly to be retired. One cottage I walk past has a postcard propped in the window offering long winter lets.

The sea is flat calm, the brown-black sand empty except for three large dogs racing around in huge circles. Their orange-clad owner calls out to them, but they're too far away to hear. At Parrog, Newport's old port, only one chimney is smoking; most of the houses are empty, the streets car-less and quiet. These days this is a pleasure beach, somewhere to tire the children and fly a kite. Fibreglass sailing boats slouch to one side where, before the bay silted up, slates, herring, wool and wine would have been heaved off wooden decks. The quiet is broken by the distant sound of a jet passing overhead, venturing out into the Atlantic.

Cat Rock and Cwm yr Eglwys

Only the belfry remains of the church in Cwm yr Eglwys, the rest destroyed by catastrophic storms.

My plan today is to walk along the coast path to Lower Fishguard, the best part of a day's journey. 'CLIFFS KILL!', warns the sign on the first wooden gate, but so far in my experience it's the path that's treacherous, not the cliffs. The mud and rock slalom that I experienced on the way to Newport is now joined by black ice. This path is determined to finish me off.

Now past Cat Rock, a curious projection into the sea only just clinging to the land, I then drop down into Cwm Rhigian where its narrow sides open into the bay of Aber Rhigian. I descend the steep cliff path to the empty pebble beach; were it not so bitterly cold, this sheltered bay would be a wonderful place to have a quick dip. I can hear the traffic speeding along the main Fishguard road – this is one of the few places where the coast path and the road come close together. To the side of the path a few acres have been planted with saplings – just a few feet tall, their tender branches are weighed down by frost. The gradient of the headland and the steep drop off to the sea means that the sun won't reach the shadowed coast path to defrost its thick ice.

The path now joins the county road downhill, past some cottages clinging to the slope. Even in my walking boots with their meaty tread I walk half on the grass verge to avoid going skidding on the ice. At the bottom of the hill, in the most sheltered wooded valley, stands one of the highlights of this stretch of the coast – the ruined, roofless church of Cwm yr Eglwys and its graveyard. Today it stands virtually on the shore, though it was once further away from the encroaching waves. As at Nevern, this is another church named after St Brynach. Only the belfry and part of the west wall remain of the twelfth-century building – the rest was destroyed in the Great Storm of 1859, which also claimed the *Royal Charter* and 113 other ships along the Welsh coast. This tragedy is remembered in a striking monument in the form of a typical nineteenth-century sailing boat, made by local blacksmith Eifion Thomas. What survived of the original church was further attacked by another violent storm in 1979. The headstones in the graveyard, made from poor Pembrokeshire stone and slate, are almost too smooth to read, worn down by the salt. Behind the car park in the lee of the hill some mobile homes squat in a herringbone pattern beside the tallest trees I've seen for miles.

Dinas Island

At Dinas Island, the peninsula that guards the end of Newport Bay, you can choose either to walk around the headland or to take the short cut straight across the fields. I'm beginning to wish I had done the latter, since the lower coast path clings precariously to the edge and is shaded at this time of the year; the higher route offers a more panoramic view and sunshine on your face. They call Dinas an island but it's firmly part of the mainland – once upon a time, however, it was cut off a couple of times a day by the incoming tide. A stone's throw away from me, the skipper of a blue-hulled day boat moored just off the cliffs is hauling in his pots – no doubt he's thrilled that at the end of November the sea is still so calm and bountiful.

Walking towards Dinas Head I pass Pig y Baw and then walk towards Carreg John Evan and Needle Rock. I can hear a tractor screeching across a distant field at Dinas Farm. There are caves below my feet all along this stretch of the coast. I am walking towards the shrine that drew the ancient pilgrims this way from Holywell and Bardsey Island to St David's Cathedral. Even for the less religiously inclined there is something spiritual about this place – it's a combination of the light, the sound of the sea and the landscape. The gentle mountains guarding this narrow strip of land before it falls into the sea, the springs and standing stones, must in a more godly age have seemed like the path to salvation. Even if you don't share the devotion of these pilgrims, it's easy to see why they came to the peninsulas and islands of West Wales.

Viewed from Pen-y-Fan, the rocky outcrop that is the tip of Dinas Island, the coastline stretches out in either direction like a wide tapestry. Miles away I can see a huge white ferry in Fishguard harbour, its passengers queuing on the quayside in toy cars. Their Irish Sea crossing will be more like a Mediterranean cruise today – quite a difference to the sea of a couple of days ago. Behind the long breakwater, Strumble Head reaches into the blue sea. Looking back along the coast towards Newport I feel a quiet sense of achievement at the full distance I've already covered today – until I read the map and realize how much further I still have to walk.

I'm now heading back downhill towards the crevice that hides Pwllgwaelod. When I get there, I see that the pub is open, but if I stop for a pint now the rest of this walk will be all the harder. A blackboard tied to a post offers prawn, lobster and crab sandwiches, and from the full car park it seems there are plenty of takers. On the sand opposite, a couple take it in turns to throw a ball for their dog – who looks disappointed at the short length of the beach, since it's not much more than a lob from one side to the other. Close to the water's edge a driver nervously reverses down the slipway to hook a trailer to a dingy floating in a couple of feet of freezing water – friends in wetsuits wait to lift the hull.

Climbing up the hill you can look back over the low valley floor that makes Dinas an island. The contrast between this beach, facing the full force of the Atlantic, and Cwm yr Eglwys, tucked just behind the headland, couldn't be more marked. Depending on which way the wind is blowing, one of the bays is always sheltered. At a stile at the top of the hill a walker heading in the opposite direction stops for a breather and sits heavily on the cross timber. He tells me that Fishguard is a good three hours' walk from here. I should have had that pint. It's curious the camaraderie of walkers. We are a cheery lot, unafraid to engage in conversation in the middle of nowhere in a way that we would never do in a city or a town. However, we don't feel obliged to say too much: it is the solitude of the walk that's the great prize.

The calm bay at Pwllgwaelod offers some respite from the Atlantic winds.

The path leaps sideways from the cliff top into wide fields and a high hedge hides the ocean for a while. A fat hen pheasant is as startled as me when it bolts out of the undergrowth just in front of my face.

Throughout its many miles the coast path meanders though villages and towns, past front gardens and backyards, but none of its detours is quite as surreal as the journey though Fishguard Bay Caravan Park. Fortunately it is deserted and my unease at feeling like a trespasser encroaching on someone else's holiday diminishes as I plod past each miniature garden and window. They are mostly static caravans, some of

PIRATES!

*F*our cannon look out to sea from their ruins on Castle Hill high above Lower Fishguard. In 1779 a privateer vessel, the **Black Prince**, demanded a ransom of £1000 to return a captured local ship. Although Fishguard was a prosperous trading town, it was essentially unprotected from an opportunist attack. Never a community to hand over money lightly, the good people of Fishguard stuck to their principles and refused to negotiate. The **Black Prince** fired its guns, blew up a couple of houses and damaged St Mary's Church. All of which resulted in the construction of Fishguard Fort. When it was completed in 1781 it boasted eight powder guns manned by invalids from Woolwich Arsenal. When the French force appeared off the coast in 1797 the warning gun was fired from here.

them done up with low retaining walls and wishing wells. I hope it's all bolted down well; you'd rock yourself awake here in a heavy storm.

A few fields further along, I come across a paddock with perhaps a hundred mountain ponies. In the summer they live high in the Preselis, but in the winter they come down here in search of bracken. They run after each other, playful and skittish in the wind, their unkempt manes flying. I'm a mile from Lower Fishguard now and journey's end – at least for this evening.

Beyond the headland that hides Goodwick, the long breakwater flashes its green light more prominently as the evening falls. The ferry that I could see earlier has long gone and the orange twinkling lights on the terminal road welcomes early passengers for the night crossing still hours away.

Lower Town below me is deeply shadowed at the foot of the valley, making the short days of winter even shorter. An impossible pink takes hold of the sky, a colour so vivid that you wouldn't believe it if you saw it in a painting. Strumble Head, tomorrow's destination and a whole day's walk away, lies enticingly on the horizon. I look down at my waterproof trousers to see that they are caked from foot to thigh in the mud of a day's walking; my prospects of flagging down a taxi to take me back to the cottage near Newport for the night won't improve until it gets darker.

 *Fishguard*

It's early in the morning and I'm back in Fishguard's Lower Town. The boatyard is crammed with vessels seeing out winter on the safety of dry land. When it's warmer in a couple of months or so the air will be full of electrical whirring and the smell of turpentine as the boat maintenance season begins once more. This is distinct from the sailing season in that no waterborne activity is involved – merely tinkering and pottering, including sanding the hull before applying antifouling, greasing the trailer and stripping and oiling the outboard engine. All these routines are as strictly observed as a church service, and in the countless weekend hours spent painting and dreaming, many Welsh marriages are saved. Until then the boatyard is a quiet maritime mausoleum of discoloured yachts and scruffy fishing boats waiting for spring.

A squadron of gulls raucously scavenge on the River Gwaun at low tide. On the bank at the entrance to the harbour road in front of the crouched cottages a huge rock holds a modern

artwork called *Fishguard Herrings*, placed there in memory of Lower Town's once-considerable industry. Beside it, a tiny plaque commemorates the filming of Dylan Thomas's *Under Milk Wood* in 1971 when Lower Town stood in as Llareggub – the fictional Welsh seaside town that spells 'bugger all' backwards.

I'm taking a short wander to the end of the quay closest to the sea, where Portsmouth's *Southern Star* sits high in the water. It's running its inboard diesels at full power to be certain of deep-sea reliability. Oblivious to the screaming engine and the plumes of white smoke belching from the protesting motor, the skipper fixes ropes and chains, waiting for his crew before casting off to fill the belly of his empty trawler. The more modest day boats and crabbers look on almost enviously at the start of his long voyage into the ocean.

The walk up the hill to the main town of Fishguard is a steep and winding haul, but offers a splendid view back across Lower Town. The houses clutching onto the cliff top and the sides of the road have the best view of the sea. These three-storey buildings are grand and beautifully built, though the private houses have given way to restaurants, bed and breakfasts and small hotels with long gardens reaching back to the water.

I've decided to stop in the town square for a while, if for no other reason than to recover after walking up the hill. St Mary's Church is open, so I pop in – its insides are bathed in cobalt blue from the sunlight striking the stained glass above the balcony. However, it is the graveyard that I am

Early morning in the harbour in Fishguard Lower Town, the boats stranded on the sand banks.

Welcoming the Cunard liner
Mauretania *at Fishguard Harbour, August 1909*

particularly keen to see, since it is here that Jemima Nicholas, the Welsh heroine, is remembered. Jemima boldly marched to meet the French invaders who landed in Pembrokeshire in 1797. She died, her tombstone says, in 1832 aged 82 years. On the other side of the cemetery is the grave of William Morgan – 'he died in the Thames by the unsettling of a boat aged 21 years in 1844'.

The other sides of the pretty square are occupied with the town hall, the Abergwaun Hotel and the Royal Oak – allowing the usual sins to be committed with salvation close at hand. The inn saw the signing of the French surrender in the last invasion of Britain. A large number of the shops and houses near the town centre are for sale – like so many towns on the distant edge of Wales, this once-prosperous port seems to be struggling this winter.

Goodwick

Goodwick is a short walk downhill from Fishguard's centre. Just before the hill drops towards the ferry port I spy its two huge breakwaters that stretch far out into the water, slowing the waves before they roll into the harbour. The little fishing village was transformed in the 1890s to take the Irish Sea railway traffic that had been using Neyland in South Pembrokeshire. It still runs a busy service to Rosslare, though these days its customers tend to be car and lorry drivers. When it was built, it was hoped that Goodwick would become a major transatlantic liner terminal for vessels bound for New York. For a few years the town saw ships of famous lines such as Cunard and Blue Funnel steaming off the Pembrokeshire coast, but in the end it was Southampton and Liverpool that won the race for Britain's liners. Goodwick is about to change its shape again, a hundred years after those two huge breakwaters were built, with the addition of a 500-berth marina.

I've sailed around the coast of Wales, and this stretch of the country is not well provided for when it comes to small-craft facilities. If you're in a small boat, Milford Haven to the south and far-distant Aberystwyth to the north are the nearest hides should the weather turn nasty. The marina will be a welcome facility for sailors on the west coast in need of a shower and safe anchorage.

After the relative shelter of the streets of Fishguard, Goodwick is wide open to the wind blowing straight off the sea. We've had a couple of days of freezing weather, though no snow yet, and the wind is bitterly cold. I don't mind the plunging temperatures so long as it remains dry for my last stretch of coast. Looking back I see that I've left the Preselis far behind me; they are shrouded in cold light, pink and blue. Up the very steep hill behind the ferry terminal the coast path winds through the east-facing Harbour Village, an old housing estate with the best views back to Newport and Fishguard. The houses were built for the port and railway workers serving a once rapidly expanding harbour.

Looking down at the harbour, a dredger breakfasts on sand and behind it a ferry slows at the sight of land and turns hard before its berth. The car drivers parked in a line waiting for their ship to come in won't have seen her yet.

To the side of the ferry terminal, six men in orange jackets are clearing the railway line of overhanging branches and twigs. This is the end of the track that crosses Britain from Paddington. I used to come home on the train from London and could once recite all the stations so familiar from the announcements at every station; Reading, Swindon, Bristol Parkway, Newport, Cardiff, all change for stations to Fishguard 'arbour. Door to door, the journey took up to seven hours: two from London to Cardiff and five across Wales, changing at Swansea or Carmarthen, then dawdling past estuaries and stopping to open farm gates. Beautiful, but slow.

At the end of the road at Harbour Village the houses thin out and give way to a handful of allotments, the empty climbing frames for sweet peas and runner beans holding on for dear life

---

THE LAST INVASION OF BRITAIN….

 A couple of miles outside Goodwick a standing stone on the coast path at Carregwastad Point marks the last land invasion of Britain, by the French in 1797. Today's headline writers with an eye for a story probably would have summed it up as: 'Drunk Frogs seen off by Cross-Dressing Fishguard Birds'. Three French frigates anchored off shore here and landed a rabble of 1400 convicts under the command of the 70-year-old Irish American General Tate. Against the backdrop of the French Revolution he planned to stir the peasantry of Pembrokeshire and unshackle them from their yokes. He set up his headquarters at Trehowel Farm, which was stocked ready for a wedding. (Following in a long tradition of Pembrokeshire weddings, much drunkenness and a fight ensued.) After initial confusion, the Earl of Cawdor mobilized Pembrokeshire's finest and

eventually brought the invaders to heel. However, one twist in the tale is that some of the French soldiers may have mistaken some Welsh women standing on the cliffs in their traditional tall black hats and red cloaks for Grenadier Guards – leading to the soldiers' quick surrender!

One unlikely heroine of the hour was Jemima Nicholas, who single-handedly captured 12 Frenchmen armed only with a pitchfork, for which she was awarded a pension of 50 pounds for the rest of her long life. What this says about the physical qualities of Jemima or her French captives is left to your imagination – personally, I always think of Hattie Jacques as Jemima versus an army of Charles Hawtreys. Whatever actually happened in 1797, the colourful legend lives on in Pembrokeshire. In 1997 the townsfolk of Fishguard produced a tapestry to commemorate the bicentenary.

in the windiest plot in Pembrokeshire. The mud on the path is frozen brick hard. I can hear a motorbike screeching its way around Goodwick, its exhaust baffle removed to attract attention – sounds travel far on such a cold day.

The ferry has slowed its speed now, there's no bow wave as it plods its way across a cold calm channel. There are no passengers outside on deck enjoying their arrival; it's too cold and they're staying behind glass in the warm for their last few minutes at sea.

In 1941 the Irish ferry heading for Fishguard was sunk by the Luftwaffe during the Second World War. The *St Patrick* had left Rosslare and was about 12 miles from Strumble Head when the German bombers intercepted her. The previous summer she had been attacked but had reached port safely. This time there was no escape. The Fishguard lifeboat searched throughout that morning but found nothing. Later, however, news reached the port that the majority of the people on board had been rescued and landed at Milford Haven. Seventeen of her crew, a gunner and 12 passengers were lost – the ferry having sunk within five minutes of the attack. Among those who died was the ship's captain, Jim Faraday, and his son Jack, a Merchant Navy officer cadet who had decided to accompany his father.

Strumble Head

The delightful thing about Pembrokeshire is its extraordinary contrasts: you can scramble down the steps at St Govan's in the south of the county and stare bewitched at the tiny hermit's chapel at the foot of the rocks, and then a few miles later watch a line of supertankers navigating their way into Milford Haven. It's the same with Strumble Head, which couldn't be further removed from the sprawl of the town so close by. Fishguard can be rather boisterous and earthy – it has all the right ingredients

TO THE LIGHTHOUSE

Strumble Head Lighthouse sits on Ynys Meicel, St Michael's Island. A small island, I grant you, but an island nonetheless, connected to the mainland by a little bridge. The lighthouse was built over 100 years ago to caution and guide the growing traffic from Fishguard on one of the most treacherous stretches of coastline in Britain. During the nineteenth century alone some 60 vessels came to grief in these waters. The engineering is remarkable – with its giant chains, outsize wheels and small portholes, not unlike the inside of a ship; its confined spaces are rammed full of over-engineered mechanics built to last forever. The clockwork rotating lamp sitting in a bowl of mercury didn't need its mechanism to see out the century – it was electrified in the 1960s – to the great relief no doubt of the men who had to wind it every twelve hours, but in an age when even a domestic fridge gives up after a few years, Strumble Head's lighthouse is a shining testament of beautiful and enduring craftsmanship.

I clambered up the lighthouse years ago for a television outside broadcast – the same difficult position that taxed the builders in 1908 challenged the BBC's engineers too; the lighthouse is built on a rock separated from the mainland by only a few feet but that chasm looks down into a demonic washing machine of treacherous sea. The stonemasons used a block and tackle to swing their equipment and materials into place when they built it.

for a good night out – and then just a few miles away you find yourself on this windswept bleak moorland dominated by the old volcano of Garnwnda, looking down on treeless farms, narrow lanes, small fields and high hedges. Aside from a collection of rusting Morris Minors in a field, the landscape has remained unchanged for a century. It's a world away and lost in another age.

As I'm passing a little whitewashed cottage called Penrhyn, right by the side of the coast path, I catch sight of the occupant standing at the sink in her Marigolds washing the cups and saucers. What is the etiquette on the coast path upon seeing strangers at close proximity in their homes? Should one wave – or pretend that one hasn't seen each other? The cottage is one of those homes that began life as a modest low box and then grew sideways, sprouting smaller boxes as Pembrokeshire cottages do. Clinging to the cliff above the Irish Sea it has one of the most perfect settings imaginable, yet like so many Pembrokeshire houses it's built with its back to the ocean to protect it from the blast. The big windows are on the other side of the house looking towards the fields. The kitchen and the bathroom have the best views of the sea. A crowd of us stayed in this cottage one New Year – if you ever have the good fortune to stay there, the warmest bed is in the crog loft, since it gets the heat from the front room's fire below.

Whether you are at sea or on a long walk, there is something comforting about seeing a lighthouse. I suppose it is the affirmation of where you are and where you are not. I have sailed past this coast in the small hours and known from my chart that somewhere soon on the horizon a white dot in the darkness will quieten my growing anxiety. Lighthouses are the truths by which mariners live. By night and seen from the water, the entire coast from St David's to Barmouth can look very similar, since there are no bright lights or distinguishing landmarks. It is the sweep of this lighthouse that draws the signposts in darkness and marks out the miles. It is the same walking the coast path: for the past few days Strumble Head lighthouse has stood out in the distance, marking my journey's end. Like some whitewashed Greek monastery clinging to a cliff, it stands aloof from the comings and goings of all below. There is no one at home these days, no jaunty lighthouse keeper welcoming visitors, pipe clenched in teeth – they've all gone now, replaced by some computer in far-off Harwich.

A few walkers togged up with mittens and mufflers to protect their faces from the cold wander ahead of me in the same direction. Even on a bitter day it's almost mesmeric to stand beneath the squat little tower and watch the four flashes every 15 seconds – you can see them up to 26 miles away.

Thirty miles after I began walking at St Dogmaels I don't want to stop now – after all, the path goes on to wind its way around the peninsulas of St David's and Castlemartin before coming to an end in Amroth in the south of the county. Tomorrow I will miss the roll of the waves and their crash onto the shore – they have been constant companions in recent days.

One day I will walk the coast path's entire length from north to south simply to be able to say that I have done it. Walking slowly past farms and fields allows you to get under the skin of a place. Not having completed the entire coast path is one of those things that will be at the back of my mind until I walk it all. There are kinder months to wander this coast – the spring and summer would have seen carpets of wild flowers showing the way – but in the bleakness of winter with all its coldness and cruelty I have seen another side to Pembrokeshire to treasure. Elated to have walked so far, seen so much, stand at the cliff's edge and stop and look out at the sea, I can't help feeling that nothing else will quite measure up to these past few days. I've travelled all over the world to every continent and many countries but have never found anywhere on earth that instils such a sense of inner peace. It doesn't have the sophistication of cities or the warmth of deserts but it has an indefinable magnetism that will always draw me back.

Cardiff

PENARTH HEAD ⚬ CARDIFF BAY ⚬ PIERHEAD

BUILDING ⚬ SENEDD ⚬ NORWEGIAN CHURCH ⚬

WALES MILLENNIUM CENTRE ⚬ MILLENNIUM

STADIUM ⚬ CASTLE ARCADE ⚬ CENTRAL MARKET ⚬

CIVIC CENTRE ⚬ CARDIFF CASTLE ⚬ BUTE PARK

*I*T'S ALL too easy for us to overlook that which we have on our doorsteps, to take for granted what we see every day. Wales is a foreign country to many people in England, but plenty in Wales don't explore close to home either. I visited the islands off the Welsh coast a few years back and was astonished to meet so many people who lived in mainland towns and villages overlooking Flat Holm, Caldey and Bardsey who'd never dreamt of visiting them.

I've lived in Cardiff for 15 years but I've never really done the tourist thing, and never really looked hard at this place that is my adopted home. You have different needs of a city when you live and work in it. Anyway, it's about time I took a closer look at the Welsh capital.

It's early on a cold grey Friday in March, and I'm standing on Penarth Head, just outside Cardiff; it's too cold to keep your hands outside your pockets for long, but the emerging sun offers some hope of warmth. The sound of the breeze slapping the masts of Penarth Marina's yachts creates a monotone orchestra; few of these boats will see their sails hoisted this morning. On the River Severn side of the enormous Barrage that keeps the sea out of Cardiff Bay's fresh water, the river is the colour of weak tea from the earth washed down in the retreating tide. This is almost the end of the journey for Britain's mightiest river, which begins life in a mist-shrouded bog in Plynlimon, 2000 feet up in the Cambrian Mountains of Mid Wales. After such modest and unpromising beginnings the Severn tumbles and turns 220 miles, flirting with the English counties of Shropshire, Worcestershire and Gloucestershire before finding the Atlantic in this final flourish, this massive muddy estuary five miles wide.

The River Severn defines a clear boundary between South Wales and England. In North and Mid Wales the border with our neighbour pretty much follows the ancient line of Offa's Dyke, though on a car journey through those northern lanes you can easily slip back and forth between the two countries without noticing, only the occasional bilingual road sign or a Welsh place name giving the game away. But here in South Wales, we have this mighty, natural barrier

OPPOSITE: The iconic
Pierhead Building,
a reminder of Cardiff's past
glory and wealth.

between the two nations. The river and its estuary form a proper border and you know when you have crossed it.

Outside the Barrage wall I've sailed up the Severn in a yacht and felt the power of its tide grab the rudder and play with the hull like a toy boat in the bath. The first time it happens, the colour drains from your face – choosing the wrong time to sail upriver is like throwing a ball up a hill. Increasing the engine's throttle is next to useless. To attempt to travel up the Severn by boat is to reach back in time and understand the fearsome obstacle that this stretch of water presented to centuries of travellers. It's one of those journeys that forces you to acknowledge the power of the natural world, even in an age of motors and satellites – a humbling voyage where your safe passage is in the gift of the currents.

On the shore here at Penarth Head, beneath the horizontal layers of geological time laid bare in the cliff face, a handful of teenage anglers wait beside an unpromising sea for the chance of a fish. Some wear hoodies, others combat fatigues; all of them are half-frozen in the cold wind. The wooden groynes that stretch from the waves to the cliffs mark convenient territory for each angler. After casting, there begins the long wait for a tug on the line. Even among friends it's too cold to talk much, and after watching the plop of the weight and its place in the tide, each angler retreats up the stones to sit uneasily on his bait box and stare into the muddied waters.

Cardiff Bay Barrage at Penarth Head has stopped the tide from ever going out.

From here across the river you can see the long low sweep of the English coast and in the channel between two countries is the lump of rock that is

CROSSING THE SEVERN

Those of my grandparents' generation, before the Severn was bridged, were used to detours. Back then the road journey from South Wales to England meant a queue of Austins and Rileys cooking quietly at Beachley while waiting for the ferry. If it was too rough for the ferry to sail, then you had to detour to Gloucester, where the Romans had built their ford. Either way, a travel rug, flask and sandwiches were essential travelling companions. Back then it must have felt as if you were travelling a long way to another country.

The river that stalled travellers for thousands of years has been tamed now, its might neutered and its powers diminished. First it was the railway tunnel, opened in 1886, which took 14 years to dig under the riverbed. It's still used today for the main railway connection to South Wales. The ferry was established as a regular service during the first day of the 1926 General Strike. Then, 40 years later, the first cars crossed the Severn Bridge. Since 1996 there's been the Second Severn Crossing to help take the strain of the traffic off the first bridge. Now millions of drivers never have to figure out tides, ferry timetables or plan elaborate detours. From their car windows high above the bullying currents, the Severn looks pretty and impotent, and all over in a moment.

Flat Holm Island, the most southerly point in Wales. Flat Holm has been a Viking anchorage, the supposed burial ground of the murderers of Thomas Becket, one-time cholera hospital and the place where Marconi's first radio signal was received, though the inventor sent his assistant George Kemp to battle the ferocious tides while he stayed on the mainland at Lavernock Point.

Behind the island's whale-like hump, Clevedon and Weston-super-Mare cling to the brooding English coastline that looms in the distance. In summer, boats will carry day trippers from Wales to England, but this early in spring the voyage into open water would be something of an ordeal. A stone's throw from where I'm standing at the end of the Barrage wall, a long line of buoys marks the route up to the entrance to Cardiff Bay's lock gates.

Behind me on the edge of the Barrage a handful of passengers wait for the AquaBus, a regular service that ferries tourists around Cardiff's waterways. The boat takes an hour or so to chug around a circuit that begins here then heads across the water to Cardiff Bay, up the River Taff past Brain's Brewery and the Millennium Stadium, and then on to Bute Park and Cardiff Castle. I've never jumped on the AquaBus before, and for a city that built its success on the water, what better way to explore Cardiff?

 *Taking to the Water*

Our tour boat appears in the distance, accelerating towards us; it looks like a white single-deck bus with a glass roof. The scraggle of waiting passengers pick up shopping bags and knapsacks and in the most British fashion order themselves into an honest queue. As the boat draws near, I notice that all the seats are empty – we are the first passengers of the day. The two crewmen look relieved to see a small gathering waiting expectantly as they draw alongside the new, wooden jetty bolted onto the enormous old stone quay.

Penarth's grand yet faded Customs House, which was built in the 1860s, looks down on the AquaBus in contempt. This was once one of the busiest ports in the country, and the rooms of the Customs House would have been filled with bustling captains; today its huge windows offer a magnificent view of the marina for its new customers – the diners in a restaurant. The building next door to the Customs House, equally grand and from the same period, is empty and boarded up. Its blind eyes must once have had the best view in Penarth.

Our tour boat moves off Penarth Head with a judder. The engines purr and the bow turns to point towards the distant jetty poking out from the restaurants at Mermaid Quay. This will not be a long voyage. Our skipper settles back into his seat and pushes the throttle gently. The flat water parts before us and the chatter on board dies down as the passengers become mesmerized by the hull's swish and the engine noise.

So many ships' crews must have given heartfelt thanks to see this view after a voyage across oceans. Cardiff meant journey's end, payment and all the salacious delights that docks could offer. In the distance across the water the cathedral-like Pierhead Building, with its red pointing spires, and behind it the low shadow of the mountains, look like painted scenery from a school play. For generations of travellers before the age of road and rail, this was the front door to Cardiff, what you saw when you arrived and departed. Scott must have looked back at this skyline when he sailed from Cardiff on the *Terra Nova* in 1910, headed for the South Pole. There are plaques dedicated to his memory in one of the city's parks, in the coal exchange, and near the quay where the vessel was moored. His name is also remembered in a bar on the waterfront.

A sailboat leaving Cardiff docks with the Pierhead Building in the background.

To sail right up to the quay in Cardiff the tide needed to be just right, of course. This was once a muddy port on a stretch of water that experiences one of the world's greatest tidal ranges. It's the funnel shape of the Severn Estuary that squeezes the water to such heights and speeds. Before they built the Barrage across what is now known as Cardiff Bay, effectively forming a huge pond, ships had to loiter in deeper water waiting for high tide. These docks could only be used for a few hours a day either side of high water. Like the Severn's tunnel and bridges, here, too, the river has been tamed and changed.

The Pier Head
Cardiff

The construction of the Barrage was the final piece in the regeneration of this area. Cardiff had grown rich on steel and coal, turning it into a major commercial port; when the demand for coal fell, so too did the fortunes of the city. The twentieth century saw the slow decline of Cardiff, until it was decided to give the area a boost with the building of a leisure and tourist community by the sea. In place of the dwindling and disappearing cargoes of heavy industry that forged Wales's place in the world, the new industries

CARDIFF'S BLACK GOLD

*T*here's been a settlement where Cardiff stands since Roman times, but for centuries the town remained modest. What is most remarkable about Cardiff's story is its explosion in size and population. Part of its great fortune was related to its location on the water. But Cardiff was also sitting in the largest continuous coalfield in Britain, one thousand square miles of mountains and valleys from Pembrokeshire to Gwent. It wasn't just the size of the coalfield that made it significant but also the type of fuel. Anthracite, the oldest and deepest coal, found in the western coalfield, was used for firing furnaces and stoves. Steam coal from the middle area offered little smoke and hot fire for ships and trains, while bituminous coal from the eastern parts found close to the surface was prized for open grates.

This coal was instrumental in powering the Industrial Revolution in South Wales. Swansea at one point produced 50 per cent of the world's copper supplies, and by the early nineteenth century Merthyr was the iron capital of Britain. As much as 40 per cent of Britain's iron came from South Wales, and aside from coal to shape it they needed a port to export it. Cardiff's greatest resource, however, were the high-quality steam coal reserves. These were barely touched until much later; peak production was reached in 1913 at 56 million tons.

The enormous improvements in transport networks that fanned out from these docks helped drive the success of the city. In 1798 the countryside between Cardiff and Merthyr was dug out to build the Glamorgan Canal, linking the great iron town with the sea. Fifty locks over a distance of 25 miles sped the journey to market. Not so far away, Richard Trevithick ran his first locomotive at Penydarren iron works in 1804. The construction of West Bute Dock in 1839 meant that vessels could be loaded and unloaded more quickly than ever before. Taff Vale Railway opened in 1841, and when the Great Western Railway linked up to South Wales in 1852 with the Midlands and London it became one of the most prosperous lines in Britain. After the construction of East Bute Dock in 1855, Roath Basin in 1887 and Queen Alexandra Dock in 1907, the coalfields of South Wales had made Cardiff one of the most important ports in the world. And as the Empire grew, so did Cardiff.

of media, tourism and the public sector would take up the slack. Where once coal and steel were loaded onto ships, now apartments, townhouses and waterside businesses sprung up. By the late 1980s the town that had been at the heart of the Industrial Revolution witnessed one of the largest engineering projects in Europe – 500 acres of freshwater lake, eight miles of waterfront and a new beginning for the quaysides lying idle.

Not everyone welcomed the transformation of this industrial wasteland and the concreting in of the sea. Naturalists in particular were horrified to see the loss of mud flats important for dozens of species of birds; householders in Cardiff prayed their houses wouldn't be flooded, and the politicians who signed the eye-watering cheques for the builders hoped that you really could persuade people that the old docks, well-known for crime and prostitution, could be a cool place to live and work. Cardiff's first waterside development in the Industrial Revolution had been built in an age before consultation; the city's next waterfront development brought howls of protest from many corners.

As I view Cardiff Bay in the distance, it seems clear to me that, in the haste to create a future, the Bay has seriously sidelined its past. The mass of high-rise flats and slab-faced offices

The elegant architecture of Cardiff Civic Centre has stood the test of time.

presumably offer stunning views of the water but for the most part do little to improve their surroundings. The approaching horizon is a jumble of ill-conceived constructions, most of which sit uneasily alongside the few beautiful historic buildings. By contrast, a mile away, in Cardiff's Civic Centre, the University, Law Courts, Museum and Art Gallery sit in well-planned and spacious splendour at the end of one of the greatest public parks in Britain. Those Victorian buildings constructed by the city's founding fathers exude confidence and purpose and still look good a century later. Cardiff Bay on the other hand – with a small handful of notable exceptions – offers unambitious design that already has the appearance of a fading shopping mall.

Cardiff is one of the most historic ports in the country. Somehow, though, we lacked inspiration in fashioning this new development and instead settled for something that was of the moment rather than design that would survive the test of time. You won't find much in the way of distinctly maritime architecture in the new flats and offices. Neither will you find any defined, recognisable Welsh influences – all the more bizarre in a country blessed with so much slate and stone, as well as forests thick with wood. It seems as if, when planning the new Cardiff Bay development, someone had a quick rummage around in the lucky dip bag and pulled out the design that said 'low rise, low cost, low brow – suitable for use in any quick-buck location'. It is as though we are uncomfortable with what we have been and where we have come from.

History has been pretty much erased from the quaysides and in its place a shiny Year Zero has been built; a new capital has been constructed to drag an old country to a new place. You won't find much in the way of old ships tied up alongside the jetties or a proud museum telling the story of King Coal, iron or the railways. There's not much reverence for the old buildings away from the waterfront that presided over selling cargoes around the world. Cardiff Bay is not a place for remembrance or romance. The occupiers of the new flats and offices are lucky people – who wouldn't want to live or work looking out at the water? But their construction is a selfish endeavour that is concerned only with the occupant's individual enjoyment of the view and not with the altruistic purpose of enriching the landscape. Cardiff Bay is as perhaps it has always been: brash, functional and of the moment. These waterside apartments and offices may be desirable, but they are certainly not inspiring – which is a shame because the Barrage itself is a piece of world-class engineering.

Our French skipper is now slowing the engines to edge us past two huge wooden stubs jutting from the water – they are the remains of an old pier at Mermaid Quay. We're stopping at a low wooden platform built for yachts and pleasure craft that has been inserted in front of the massive original stone quayside. There's a small crowd waiting to jump on the boat for the next leg of the journey up the River Taff and then on to Bute Park beside Cardiff Castle. I feel pleasantly surprised to be among tourists enjoying a sightseeing trip of my adopted home town.

I have an hour to do some exploring before the boat returns to take me up the river to the city centre. The AquaBus sets down its passengers just a few yards below the new Welsh Assembly debating chamber, the Senedd. Some foreign language students are disembarking too; one remarks to me that they're surprised that Wales's seat of government is out here and not in the city centre. I try to explain that while the politicians' debating chamber is here in Cardiff Bay, much of the civil service is in the city centre in the old Welsh Office. They look baffled.

The Senedd

In a small boat at sea level the Senedd towers above you. However, walking up the quay's stone steps it begins to look a bit more human in scale. This building with its glass walls and seemingly floating roof is the home of Wales's new devolved democracy – even if the building's back is firmly turned on Wales as it stares out to sea for inspiration. The chamber was designed to inspire a different sort of politics from that found in Westminster and so there are no stone walls and dark corners; instead it is transparent and accessible, at least in its architecture. It's also been designed to leave a light footprint on the earth. Its heating and lighting make the best use of the sun, and the toilets are flushed with rainwater. Unkind commentators point out that the hot air coming from the debating chamber is recycled too, using the aid of a magnificent wooden funnel made from Welsh oak, which sits at the heart of the building.

The architect has made an effort to represent all the regions of Wales – the floors are hewn from the slate quarries of Blaenau Ffestiniog in the north of the country while the oak panelling of the main debating chamber is sawn from the forests of Mid Wales. In fact, there was some debate about where the new institution should be built. Machynlleth in Mid Wales made a bid for it –

ABOVE AND OPPOSITE:
The eye-catching Senedd, the seat of Welsh Government crafted from traditional Welsh materials, including a striking 'funnel' made of Welsh oak.

after all it was where the first Welsh parliament was held by Owain Glyndwr in 1404. Swansea also offered to host the assembly. The original redevelopment plans for Cardiff Bay proposed that the waterside area would be united with the city centre a mile away with some sort of tram service, but that has yet to materialize and, save for the odd bendy bus and the AquaBus, Cardiff Bay remains a long way from the Civic Centre.

Unlike the Houses of Parliament in Westminster, you can turn up at the Senedd without notice and eat your sandwiches while looking down on the debating politicians. This has become an unlikely tourist attraction for visitors as much interested in its architecture as the politics. There is an informality about the Senedd that has moved politics away from ritual, even though, as the First Minister Rhodri Morgan once admitted, the proceedings can sometimes be as exciting as watching paint dry. This is a magnificent building and the temptation to stay here and 'people watch' is enormous. The view through the huge glass walls onto the waterfront with all its activity is truly delightful. Even for those who are not passionate advocates of devolution, this is a piece of architecture for all of Wales to be proud of.

Devolution in Wales was not at first enthusiastically grasped by a grateful electorate. In 1979 – the first time Wales was asked whether it wanted to govern itself – the answer was an overwhelming 'no'; and the second time, in 1997, it was a victory for devolution by the narrowest of margins. This is still a young institution, wobbly on its feet and yet to become confident and sure-footed. Much of

the work of the Welsh Assembly Government is done a few steps away from the shiny new debating chamber in a dull faceless office block. The vote for devolution wasn't wholehearted enough to go building a headquarters for the new government: public opinion wouldn't have allowed an enormous centre for politicians and civil servants to be constructed, so instead we have a compromise – this spectacular new debating chamber and some old back offices spread over the city. The new façade of a new democracy in this sometimes unambitious development is a metaphor for a country that lacks confidence and yearns for consensus, still unsure of its post-industrial role. It is as though we ran out of vision and couldn't go the whole hog. The political architecture is a fitting epitaph for the whole Cardiff Bay development: the concept was brilliant but in execution it lacks conviction – something that never could be said of Cardiff's founding fathers when they built their city centre.

Norwegian Church and Mermaid Quay

Walking back down the slate steps of the Senedd, I look out towards the Severn. There, perched on the side of the quay before the Barrage, I can see the Norwegian Church, moved from its original home nearby. Sailors, dockers and their families have worshipped here since 1866 – the author Roald Dahl was baptized here in 1916. The Norwegians left their mark on Cardiff but they were not the only nationality that flocked here in the shipping boom. Somalis, Yemenis, Spaniards, Italians, Caribbeans and Irish all helped create what was one of Britain's oldest multicultural communities. It's estimated that Tiger Bay – as they used to call this unique place – was once home to 45 different nationalities.

Either side of the Norwegian Church a boat is tied up to the quay – not the usual plastic-hulled yachts which are now part of the scenery here but a rusty old trawler (on what must surely be one of its last missions) and an old lightship used by the church as a floating café. Apart from the AquaBus this is the only large vessel in the entire bay that children can clamber aboard and feel the excitement of being at sea.

The Senedd's immediate neighbour is the grand old Pierhead Building, whose red spires I had seen from across the bay. Built by the Marquess of Bute, the owner of the port and various coalfields, it is a very clear and public statement of his enormous wealth – as well as a home to the Bute Dock Company. Its remarkable colour comes from the glazed terracotta tiles that cover the building.

By comparison with the Pierhead Building, the squat sprawl of Mermaid Quay looks cheap and thoughtless. The shops and restaurants are all the usual chains, and it lacks vision and respect for the heritage it's built upon. Too late now to remedy, I suppose. Not that the lack of decent architecture puts off the crowds, however. The sun has come out and Mermaid Quay is busy with pushchairs and children rollerblading. It's a curious mixture of people who inhabit the waterfront these days. Where crews once walked to their ships, now there are politicians, lobbyists, journalists, tourists and shoppers who would never have set foot in the docks 25 years ago. They have colonized the new apartments, bars and hotels that have sprung from the old quaysides. True, in a far corner closer to the sea (beyond the 'tidied up for the tourists' part) there is still a commercial port; but it is forestry, perishables and containers that busy the cranes now. The Port of Cardiff's utilitarian buildings are tucked behind the fence of the newly opened Cardiff Bay Coastal Park.

The crowds are testament to the most successful aspect of the planning here: that you can walk along the waterfront unbothered by cars. The entire development has been bold in

consigning traffic to the back streets, a safe distance from pedestrians. People come from all over the place to spend the day in Cardiff Bay and it has become a tourist destination in its own right. The flat, long walk is ideal for watching the speedboats and sailing dinghies – everyone's spirits are lifted near the sea. For all my disappointment at Cardiff Bay's failure to honour its past, I have a sneaking regard for the place. It's clear from the joy in the faces of people here that this is a rescue mission well done. A wasteland that had lost its purpose which was off limits to a large population on its doorstep is a now a much-loved playground.

The Norwegian Church is another reminder of Cardiff's past importance as an international port.

Wales Millennium Centre

Some tourists just off a coach are trying the doors of the armadillo-shaped Wales Millennium Centre – the country's home for the arts. Music and drama are as important to Wales as politics, if not more so. It is fitting, therefore, that the two headquarters sit side by side. This project started off as a proposal for an opera house. The Iraqi-born architect Zaha Hadid designed a beautiful prototype that was suffocated in a toxic public debate tinged with elitism and racism. Admittedly Zaha had at that time built relatively little (she was best known for a fire station in

The unforgettable façade of the Wales Millennium Centre, symbol of Cardiff's regeneration.

Germany), but in any case the architectural establishment and the local newspapers put paid to her grand plans and the city's longed-for home for the arts took a few more years to materialize.

When work on the new design by Jonathan Adams began they took the precaution of not calling it an opera house. An unashamedly Welsh building, clothed in slate, wood, steel and calligraphy, it's a fitting home to the Welsh National Opera, the BBC National Orchestra of Wales and other arts organizations. Like the Senedd next door, this is modern architecture at its most brilliant – understanding perfectly the place in which it's built, without being hidebound by heritage. Just to assuage the critics of elitism, the characters of the BBC's *Torchwood* series live underneath the front door in a fictional universe.

Cut into its brow, in huge letters, are the words IN THESE STONES HORIZONS SING – the inscription reminds me of a Greek or Roman temple. The interior of the Centre is as spectacular as its leaning lettered front. For such a small country Wales produces a disproportionately high number of performing artists – whether they are opera singers or actors. Many suggest that it's the tradition of performances at school – *Eisteddfodau* – that breeds world-class careers, but for many years the country didn't have a world-class arena to stage its own talent. That changed with this place. The fact that the building has space to breathe and is not cluttered with competing developments on its doorstep simply enhances its boldness.

Bute Street

I've decided to get away from the waterfront a bit, and so am heading up Bute Street, which takes you to the heart of the old maritime quarter. The same aristocrat who owned the coalmines and the harbour generously gave his name to the community that sprung up behind the ships. In Cardiff today the name Butetown elicits a kaleidoscope of reactions – not all of them generous. It's these scruffy backstreets that are the most honest reminder of the city's maritime history. Away from the glass and the stainless steel of the waterfront, these streets carry the story of what was once here. Many of them still reek of the edgy dock life that once loitered everywhere.

If you look up above street level you'll find some of the city's most lovely, yet unloved, Victorian buildings: forgotten banks, the offices of barely remembered shipping agents, the premises of long-dead insurers and provisioners without whom there was no voyage. The words 'Provision Curers bonded Store Merchants' still lie peeling high up on the walls near Hemmingway Street. Looking at all this, it strikes me as odd that one of these old stores hasn't been converted into a museum to tell the story of what was once here. There is a scratch open-air theme walk on the other side of the bay that tells the story of Cardiff, but its single coal wagon and lump of polished coal hardly do the story justice. Many of the historic buildings here are listed but on the market for sale or to let. The relatively cheap price of land here means it is unlikely that these old properties will find a new use when pitted against newly built offices. The usual cycle of emptiness, dereliction and then demolition is their sad but realistic fate.

The backstreets of Cardiff Bay were the business end of the coal industry. This is where the deals were done, ships hired and crews commissioned. Its elaborate architecture and proud houses are a long way from the hacking stench of the people who dug the black gold out of the ground. The wood-panelled Coal Exchange sits in a fine stone courtyard looking like a temple or a law court. This was a cathedral to commerce. Here in smoke-fugged din, traders would once have shouted across each other to secure or sell cargoes that would travel the world. The Coal Exchange is to be redeveloped, but at least in doing so the fabric of the building, if not its spirit, will be preserved. The same can't be said of so many of the historic buildings that lie empty in Cardiff Bay. Simply reviving and rehabilitating many of these grand properties seems to be beyond the developers' wit. It seems almost criminal.

All aboard the AquaBus again

I've boarded my next AquaBus and we're pulling off the quayside, reversing gently into the water, which flashes back the light of the mid-morning sun. How many men must have watched this horizon turn before them as they let go of the ropes and then watched Wales get smaller behind them?

NOSTALGIA AIN'T WHAT IT USED TO BE

You can be too misty-eyed about the past and it's usually those who didn't have to endure it who are most nostalgic. The coal that made this city great – that took the name of Wales around the world and paid for these grand buildings – was also the industry that put children, women and animals down the pits and killed too many of its workforce. It wasn't until the 1842 Coal Mines Act that boys under the age of ten and women were forbidden from going down the pit. Every peak of production was also marked with an unspeakable tragedy. Four hundred and thirty-nine colliers were killed in the Senghennydd disaster in 1913 in the industry's worst loss of life, and another generation would come to know the name of Aberfan for the deaths of 116 children and 28 adults. There are few world events that are universally known for their name – Chernobyl, perhaps Beslan's school, but Aberfan's images of dignified, numbed families waiting silently for their children to be pulled motionless from the coal slurry defines an industry that gave

so much and took too much from this small country. Some mourn the passing of the great age of coal, they lament the former social cohesion where everyone knew their place – but you never met a miner who wanted his son to follow in his footsteps.

So why did Cardiff decline as a great coal port? The First World War saw manpower shortages and loss of international markets. Post-war disputes with mine owners over wages and conditions led to the Lock Out and 1926 General Strike. Between 1921 and 1936, 231 mines closed. Cheaper foreign coal had displaced the expensive cargoes of South Wales by 1929. The 1970s saw East Bute Dock close to shipping and the number of mines dropped from 620 to 42. The Miners' Strike of 1984 was sparked by a mass pit closures programme, and by 1999 only one operational pit was left in South Wales. A story spanning more than a century and an industry that defined a country came to the end. You'll still find men in miner's hats not far from here, but now they are the museum guides at **Big Pit***.*

The famous 1950 photo of Welsh coal miners, by W. Eugene Smith.

Just off Penarth Marina a flotilla of red-sailed dinghies has taken to the water – youngsters competing in a race around marker buoys, in all likelihood. The AquaBus slows to allow them space to pass before making our way towards the mouth of the River Taff. They are a quieter bunch onboard this time – few photographs are being taken and many have bought the round-trip ticket to spend the next hour on the water without getting off.

Behind me the buildings of the waterfront are slowly disappearing as we move out into the bay again. The St David's Hotel and Spa with its sail on the roof looks slightly scruffy and older than it is. Many will be familiar with this scene since it is the backdrop to the local TV news for Wales. This is the view of itself that Wales projects to the country, cutting-edge architecture in a new waterside development removed from the encumbrances of the past. I'm never really sure how representative of Wales this image really is. We are a sometimes romantic, sometimes backward-looking nation, more comfortable with the past than the future, yet we have exchanged coalmines and steel works for call centres and insurance giants.

Suddenly our progress is halted at the point where Cardiff Bay meets the River Taff. A race marshal in an inflatable rescue boat speeds towards us to request us to stop. There is a rowing regatta on the Taff that takes precedence over all motorized vessels – the tight confines of the river won't accommodate the outstretched oars of racing rowers and another boat passing in the other direction. On a train or a bus the passengers would probably get agitated at the announcement of a 20-minute delay, but on a sunny day bobbing about on the water there's not a murmur. Beside us on the Penarth side of the river sits another brand-new waterside development of low-rise apartments. Some are sold but many have 'For Sale' signs plastered across the windows with lots of inducements to sign up.

The River Taff

Twenty minutes later we are off again and we enter the narrow channel of the Taff. The roads of Cardiff are gridlocked every morning in every direction with one passenger in each car – many of them travelling only a few miles. Yet in a city built on rivers the AquaBus doesn't start running until after the morning rush hour is over, focusing instead on tourists and sightseers. There must be thousands of people who live in Penarth and Cardiff who would jump at the chance of going to work by water taxi. It's odd that a country that built its wealth on the sea has forgotten how to use its waterways.

On the city side of the river the tall brick chimney of Brain's Brewery hoves into view. Brain's have been brewing in the city since 1882; it's this brewery that provides Cardiff's signature smell when you get off the train. There's no smell of warm hops on the wind this afternoon, however. Behind the brewery, the white tarantula-legged Millennium Stadium, the country's rugby amphitheatre, is quiet. So many cities throughout the world built their new stadia outside the centre and in exchange for easy parking and cheap land lost the atmosphere that this city's roaring stadium exudes on match afternoons.

A couple of youths standing on the road bridge drop stones on the roof of the AquaBus as we pass under, and the graffiti scrawled on the walls reminds me that however pleasant our journey, we are in the middle of urban Britain. The boat crew look bemused and embarrassed that the agreeable atmosphere of the voyage has been momentarily interrupted.

The AquaBus passes the Millennium Stadium, with its distinctive cantilevered roof.

Once again we are nearing a stop, this time Bute Park, beside Cardiff Castle. The engines slow, the crew move silently like ballet dancers to their precarious positions at bow and stern, ready to throw ropes over the jetty posts. This is the furthest large vessels can sail upriver on the Taff – the weirs ensure that the rest of the waterway is for canoeists and fishermen only. The Taf Fechan (Little Taff) and Taf Fawr (Big Taff) rise as two streams in the Brecon Beacons. They gather the Nant Morlais and Nant Rhydycar at Merthyr, then another Taff (the Taf Bargoed) and the Cynon and Rhondda rivers before arriving in Cardiff near Llandaff Cathedral.

The Taff's route through the city was altered by the construction of the railway. In the nineteenth century the iron and coal industries and the discharge of raw sewage made this one of the most polluted rivers in Wales. In 1872 a report on the river stated it was uninhabitable to wildlife, and a similar investigation in 1970 came to the same sad conclusion. The decline of heavy industry brought with it a cheering story of conservation success, and the river is now cleaner than it has been for centuries and teaming with fish again. There are a healthy number of eager anglers on both riverbanks and every so often in the water an encouraging number of leaping fish.

It's a short walk from the jetty at Bute Park to the castle and city centre. There's a tour around the rooms of Cardiff Castle on the hour and I've just missed the two o'clock by five minutes so I'm off to explore the city's old arcades and market.

The Arcades and Central Market

Indoor shopping is Cardiff's speciality, a cunning investment in a country blessed with so much rain. The hidden jewels of the city centre are the long Victorian glass-roofed arcades that shoot off from the main streets. These three-storey warrens of cafés and antique shops are a gentle delight compared to the enormous new retail centre under construction nearby. In an effort to lure out-of-town shoppers back into the city centre the St David's 2 complex promises retail heaven; however, it will never be able to compete with the arcades when it comes to intimacy and charm.

You can hear and smell Cardiff Central Market a few dozen yards before you walk into it. 'Two for a pound!', 'Fresh strawberries!' and 'Two punnets for one!' are never heard in supermarkets. The smell of fresh fish and the cries of stallholders are fitting introduction to an emporium where you can still buy parts for a discontinued vacuum cleaner or a spare hairpiece. Inside, the market looks like a railway station without any trains. Its huge hangar-like structure was built using the finest Victorian engineering and as a market it is still vibrant and successful. Split across two levels, its second tier is no more than a wide shelf of stores running around the outside wall and a perch to look down at the stalls below. This is the home of all those little shops you thought had disappeared. On the first floor near the BULL TERRIER CAFÉ, SUNDAY SCHOOL SUPPLIES, KELLY'S BARBER SHOP and CLUBS, TROPHIES & ENGRAVINGS you can look down on the busier stalls on the ground floor below. ELECTRICAL SUPPLIES and SEW ELEGANT, like their next-door neighbours, are not exactly rushed off their feet, but more than one customer at a time would mean the stallholder compromising personal service. The SECOND HAND RECORD AND DVD stall is being packed up for the day when a potential customer slows down beside a box marked 'Damaged LPs'. This is clearly the secret market known only to the cognoscenti who saunter up the stairs and know what they're looking for.

RIGHT: *Perfect for wet-weather shopping, Cardiff's enticing Arcades.*

OVERLEAF: *Cardiff Central Market, where you can find just about anything.*

The ground floor is an altogether busier affair. GRIFFITHS: Top-Quality Beef, Pork, Lamb and Poultry has a queue of shoppers, eager to get something for dinner. The pink flesh of the legs and ribs on display is matched by the wide smile in the white apron. The bread stall's stock is dwindling now – they know how much to bake. The WIG AND HAIRPIECE SHOP has two customers, both awkwardly waiting for attention – one looks young and in need of a prop for a party tonight, while the other looks as though he wishes he were just young. ASHTON'S, the legendary fish shop mentioned in hushed tones by cooks who know, are starting to hose down for the day. Lying on the ice is a bucket full of mussels, as well as turbot and salmon, shrimps, prawns and crayfish – the latter usually shipped straight to southern Europe. Chalked large on the board is: 'Fresh Lobster – just in'; alternatively a platter of off-cuts provides the essentials for a tasty fish pie. It shouldn't really be able to flourish surrounded by so many supermarkets, but there is something enduring about this place – its timeless gathering of owner-stallholders and their first-name customers will ensure that it does survive.

Cardiff Castle

I've now reached Cardiff Castle, but it's only an hour until it closes to visitors. Outside the main gate two coaches are waiting for a party of foreign students and a group of day-tripping old folks. Both parties seem reluctant to leave the sunshine of the lawn beside the road for the certain steaming heat of their transport. Inside the curtain wall the daffodils are out and the lawns at their most green. I decide to begin with the tour of the interior, so that the staff can lock up the rooms behind me.

John Betjeman was sent to Cardiff by the BBC for one of his talks broadcast in 1952. He spoke of the two worlds of Cardiff and like many visitors of the time didn't go near the docks but confined his note-taking to the castle (which bowled him over). He described the docks as 'that crowded town of coloured people cut off geographically by railways and water from the rest of Cardiff'. The Civic Centre beside the castle he thought to be the finest in these islands. Betjeman looked out from the battlements and noted that the Bute family wouldn't permit any development that might obscure their view of the city and the Severn. The Bute family is long gone now and so too their prohibition of high-rise building – today the view to the sea is blocked by concrete tower blocks, while the turrets are cowed and diminished by taller encroaching buildings. The old Bank of Wales building peers easily over the wall, watching the keep.

When Betjeman wandered around the castle on his visit he quickly got lost in the endless passageways and corridors – something that looks unlikely under the watchful eye of our guide. We begin our tour on the battlements overlooking the castle gardens beneath the ancient keep, the one-time playground of the wealthiest baby in the empire. The Marquess of Bute's family only ever lived here for six weeks of the year – this was a holiday home for a Scottish family, albeit one of the wealthiest families in the world. Their enormous mineral wealth allowed them a lifestyle that is almost beyond imagination even to this day. This was one of the first houses to be wired for electricity and central heating in the country. Although one helpful member of our tour party reminds us that all Roman villas had central heating many centuries before.

The castle is a building of two halves. The ancient keep looks as castles should: ruined and uncomplicated, and surrounded by a vast curtain wall. The modern castle, restored and improved by William Burges, is built along one of the castle walls and is no more than one room deep –

admittedly one vast room deep. Our first destination is the Gentleman's Smoking Room, heavy with ornate gilding and stacked with all the necessities for a good night in with the boys – inlaid cigar case, a generous wine cupboard and a wolf over the entrance to keep the women out.

Bedecked with fables around the walls, the Children's Day Nursery overlooking the lawn on the first floor was also home to four different nannies and governesses, who were contracted to speak only in their native tongue so that the young Bute charges would become fluent in French and Italian from an early age.

We then entered one of the most splendid rooms of the castle, the banqueting hall. Even if the family were entertaining only a few guests, they insisted on the palatial splendour of dining here. The family dining room is an altogether more modest affair, though the table has a hole cut in its centre to push through a vine – allowing diners to enjoy grapes picked straight from the plant. Dorian, our guide, also points out the carved nut in a monkey's mouth, which acts as a bell-push to summon the servants. No one came when I pressed it.

The sleeping habits of the wealthy always intrigue visitors and the guide has the audience's full attention when explaining the predilections of the master of the house. With the exception of a squabbling middle-aged Chinese couple (who seem frankly baffled by most of the tour so far), the party is captivated. It transpires that the Marquess of Bute slept in a small single bed without his wife. This revelation immediately has the Americans in our party nodding, as if it confirms all their suspicions about the British aristocracy. The bedspread made from golden thread has been removed lest the light-fingered whip out their scissors. The Marquess was also the proud owner of one of the first en suite bathrooms in Britain. At this point our party looks to our antique central heating expert, hopeful of some fresh insight – but none is forthcoming.

The newer part of Cardiff Castle seen from across the immaculate lawns.

Perched atop its motte, the medieval keep of Cardiff Castle is forbidding yet impressive.

And so to the Library, a grand affair with thousands of leather-spined volumes housed in beautifully hand-made cases positioned at right angles to the windows to save the books from direct sunlight. On closer inspection the brown and green Bible-like volumes are the minutes of the last hundred years of Cardiff Council meetings – the family removed their own collection of books when they left the castle and its new owners filled the shelves with years of the unreadable. They look the part, though; you'd never know unless you looked closely and opened their covers. This is the end of the tour of the interior, and the prospect of a Betjeman-like saunter through the cordoned-off parts of the house seems unlikely.

When we finish the tour and return outside I see that the castle grounds are still busy with young families who couldn't face the tour of the rooms and the numerous flights of stairs. The outside offers more than enough to occupy short legs for hours, principally the chance to run around in a real-life fairytale castle. It has turned out to be a glorious, sunny day, an unexpected pleasure this early in the spring. When the sun falls it will soon turn cold in the shadow of the walls, however. The clock on the Civic Centre ponderously chimes four o'clock, followed a few seconds later by the castle's own clock. It's only half an hour until the gates close, so there's just time to climb to the top of the old keep.

If you asked a child to draw a castle, this is what they would sketch – a simple octagonal tower with turrets atop a hill and a flag fluttering from the battlements. Sadly the keep, the oldest part of the castle, is covered in scaffolding for my visit. Stonemasons are busy restoring the walls –

and in some cases restoring the previous restoration. A lot of the stonework was repaired with cement and concrete in the past, and now that has to be gently hacked out and replaced with a kinder repair of lime mortar. Swarms of foreign language students have had the same thought as me and are walking quickly towards the tower clutching their audio tour guides to their heads.

Compared to the Butes' stately home on the other side of the lawn, the keep is a delightful ruin, for the most part windowless and empty. The newer house's huge windowed rooms, opulent interiors and spired roofs are a million miles from the cold dark cells that make up each floor of the keep. But the scramble to reach its open roof with its wonderful views is definitely worthwhile.

There is something of a child's delight in scaling a tall building and looking down to see how far you've climbed. Beneath the walls the last visitors of the evening, looking as small as the ducks pecking the grass for scraps, are waddling their way towards the gate and home for tea. From the top of the keep I can see the Bristol Channel and a ship sailing through it – the reason that the Romans built their lookout and stronghold here. Centuries later the Marquess could spy on his docks without having to venture far from home. Looking round I can also see the grand domed City Hall, Law Courts, Museum and University, all carved in Portland stone.

On the other side of the keep the mountains beckon. Before suburbia sprawled its way to the flood plain of the Taff, the green tablecloth was interrupted only by Llandaff's cathedral spires and the towers of William Burges's fairytale Castell Coch. Burges, who did so much to reshape Cardiff Castle itself, built Castell Coch on top of medieval remains on a hill overlooking the city. The building offers a very romantic, very nineteenth-century vision of the Middle Ages.

The gardens of Bute Park beneath us, reaching as far as the eye can see, were once the private domain of the Bute family, used for their own secluded enjoyment. This park is perhaps Cardiff's most prized treasure; its green lung reaches from the outskirts of the city, beyond Llandaff Cathedral, all the way to the castle walls. Few other cities in Britain have in the face of unceasing pressure from motorists and developers managed to keep nature so close at hand. Capability Brown's carefully managed landscape was set down in the late eighteenth century, and then further improved and altered later. It was the wealth of the Bute family that kept the houses away from the trees to bequeath one of the greatest open spaces in Wales – and all the more remarkable when the pressure to build everywhere in this fast growing city was at its most intense.

Ivor Novello was born in a terraced house to the side of Bute Park. The composer who kept wartime spirits alive with songs like 'Keep the Home Fires Burning' wouldn't have been permitted to clamber up the trees and run around the fields as a small boy. The public was admitted only on Sundays until the Butes passed over ownership of the land in the 1940s. Their iron grip extended to the leasehold of much of the surrounding architecture: the splendid three-storey houses of Cathedral Road and its adjacent terraces all owe their intricate masonry, marble fireplaces and stained glass to the Marquess and his architect.

Far beyond Glamorgan Cricket Club, the ordered trees and manicured borders give way to wide fields and less coiffeured parkland. It is here that Llandaff Cathedral stands – a safe distance from Cardiff Castle's inhabitants. Below those trees in the far distance through the graveyard the faithful will be walking to choir practice for evensong. This evening the Latin verses of Bruckner's *Christus Factus Est* will rise to the rafters. Like the castle and Cardiff Bay, the cathedral's majesty and splendour are not typical of the small chapels and hidden holy places; the real Wales lies beyond the horizon. It's time to go back to the Wales of the B-roads and byways.

CHAPTER
FOUR

The Vale of Glamorgan

ST HILARY ◉ COWBRIDGE ◉ ST QUENTIN'S CASTLE ◉

OLD BEAUPRE CASTLE ◉ PLAS LLANMIHANGEL ◉

GREAT FRAMPTON HOUSE ◉ LLANTWIT MAJOR

C ARDIFF isn't yet a densely packed city, and with large green spaces such as Bute Park perhaps it will stay that way. But for those city-dwellers who crave country life, the best direction to head is west.
There, beyond Cardiff's suburban sprawl, past the larger houses with their manicured gardens and the sprouting out-of-town retail parks, the fields and trees begin to replace the concrete and tarmac as the city slowly gives way to leafier lanes of the Vale of Glamorgan.

OPPOSITE: The rather curious-looking church in Llanmihangel.

◉

This was once the richest county in Wales, home to mine- and port-owners – much of Wales's wealth came through Glamorgan's gates en route to market. It is still one of the country's richest counties: this is where many of Cardiff's wealthier commuters live, just a short drive to the dental practice, doctor's surgery or Law Courts. The Vale of Glamorgan is a well-kept secret. Those visitors to Cardiff who escape the city's cultural and sporting attractions tend to head for the National History Museum at St Fagans; the Vale's charms are often missed by motorists flying along the M4 to the beaches of the West Wales coast, which is a shame because this area much closer to the city is well worth exploring.

Contained by the sea on one side and the mountains on the other, the Vale is a narrow stretch of land that is criss-crossed by the mainline railway, the motorway, a chain of electricity pylons and Cardiff Airport's flight path – not to mention dotted with towering television masts and Aberthaw power station. (It sometimes strikes me as a curious paradox that the identity of modern Wales was forged with a great deal of help from the television transmitters that today disfigure the landscape.) In spite of this, however, the back lanes off the main Cardiff road remain high hedged and tranquil, and in the many moments of quiet away from the noise, this is much-prized countryside that has stood up well to the pressures of development. This seems all the more remarkable considering that the usual defenders of rural life – National Park status or designation as an Area of Outstanding Natural Beauty – have never been invoked here.

The Vale offers a warren of enticing back lanes too small to be classified as B-roads – they are the ancient tracks between fields and farm no wider than the cart wheels that used to trundle

South Wales's Spiritual Heartland

Glamorgan's international prominence came with the coal industry boom but its historic importance dates from much earlier times. St Illtud's Church at Llantwit Major sent missionaries all over Britain and its scholars kept the lights burning during the Dark Ages. The monasteries at nearby Ewenny, Neath and Margam were wealthy bastions of faith and learning. This was once a heartland for spiritual Wales but also land that was strategically important for security. This was the lookout post over the uncertainties of the Bristol Channel – Glamorgan was the meeting point of England's hinterland, Wild West Wales and its mountainous and unruly north. The rash of castles across the country is indicative of the need to protect wealth in uncertain times but also symbolic of a troubled land whose people lived in expectation of violence.

beside the hedgerows. Littered with ancient churches, forgotten castles and quiet battlefields, the Vale lacks the scale of the wilderness of Snowdonia in the north or the nearer Brecon Beacons. Instead it offers country life without too many of the usual rural deprivations. (You won't have to drive for an hour without seeing a soul to buy a loaf of bread as you might in Powys.) What's more, considering the endless boundary changes in Wales – the continued disappearance and reappearance of much-loved county names – it would be understandable if the sense of identity here had been diminished. But Glamorgan has a passionately held sense of pride and place that has been safeguarded by the farming community.

The town of Cowbridge, depicted here in 1860, has not forgotten its farming background.

A walk down the high street in Cowbridge on a Saturday morning might make you think that well-heeled commuters have displaced the original community, but many farmers remain in the Vale and few journeys around

here pass without reversing up a lane for a tractor coming in the other direction. Behind well-kept stone walls at the end of unsigned tracks you'll find vineyards and racing stables and country piles that you never knew were there (owned for the most part by people who want to keep it that way). The historic wealth of the farms is visible even today; the quality of the land has always been able to pay for impressive farmhouses and outbuildings – unlike the more modest dwellings of those scraping a living in poorer pastures further north and west of here.

St Hilary

I've decided to begin my exploration of the Vale in the small village of St Hilary. Sitting just off the main road from Cardiff to Cowbridge (which owes its origins to the Romans), St Hilary nestles beneath tall trees. As I turn off the main road to the village, I'm transported back to a time when the built environment was only as high as the tallest trees – St Hilary's church tower would have been the loftiest structure on the landscape. The tower has long since been dwarfed by a red-eyed television transmitter standing in a field in the far distance.

From here I can almost see the coastline of the Vale of Glamorgan – its cliffs covered in squawking gulls are a much-loved and well-documented destination, attracting a good many local visitors walking their dogs and family outings on Sunday. For my money, though, it is away from the tourist trail a few fields inland that Glamorgan hides its real treasures, along these sleepy lanes and beside dozing woodlands.

As I wander round St Hilary, it strikes me how well it fits the mould of 'quintessential country village', the perfect British rural idyll; a thatched pub, the village green, stone and slate cottages preserved in aspic and nothing too horrible from the twenty-first century. With its

The church of St Hilary, the heart of the village of the same name and home to several wonderful medieval monuments.

honey-coloured stone and low-walled cottages gathered around a squat church you could easily mistake St Hilary for the Cotswolds – Bourton-on-the-Water, perhaps, or Stow-on-the-Wold. There, however, St Hilary would be overrun by coachloads of day trippers – whereas being in Glamorgan, it's as quiet as the grave. This may be because I'm sitting under a tree outside the churchyard.

Somewhere behind the well-clipped hedges and immaculate lawns, a dog begins to bark incessantly, interrupting the birdsong. But this is not the place where you'd knock on the door and complain to your neighbours: a silent scowl from behind the Sunday supplement and fantasy of poisoning are more appropriate.

The churchyard is in full bloom this morning. The ash and chestnut trees look wonderful and the grass has been recently mown. Beyond the kissing gate, the more legible gravestones reveal a mixture of Glamorgan's great and good, as well as some of the county's more modestly departed. Some are ornate, elaborate creations, decorated in deep relief and ornate lettering. Others are simply a flat stone in the earth, the name rubbed out by the rain. Among the shorn daisies they are all equal.

The two-storeyed cottages at the edge of the graveyard would once have housed farm workers and their families, but rural labourers would be pushed to live here now. One of the chocolate box cottages is for sale this week in the local newspaper priced at three quarters of a million pounds. The post-war former local authority houses on the other side of the graveyard may be lighter on the wallet but this remains an exclusive enclave of the wealthy.

The church of St Hilary itself has all of the expected features of a village church in any well-to-do parish: a squat tower, extensions built upon extensions, intricate carvings, later stained glass windows, and a graveyard sheltered from the worst of the storms that hit the Welsh coastline. But this has none of your usual congregation-in-decline weariness about it.

In the porch I stop to look at the rotas for reading the lesson, visiting the sick and elderly, cleaning brasses and arranging the altar flowers. They are typed so neatly that I suspect they have taken as

MEDIEVAL MONUMENTS

The church of St Hilary has two medieval monuments of particular interest. Lying in a recess in the north wall of the nave is the effigy of a layman, believed to be a member of the De Cardiff family, lords of the manor of St Hilary in the twelfth and thirteenth centuries. The youth wears a long plain tunic and round-toed, peaked shoes; in his right hand he holds a pair of gauntlets. His long hair curls around his ears and is kept off his face by a band across his forehead. It is at once peaceful and humble.

His neighbour couldn't be more different. The effigy of Thomas Bassett of Beaupre, who died in 1423, is decidedly grand; he appears dressed in a suit of armour, his head propped on cushions and a sword at his side. His splendour has been defaced with the passing of time – perhaps some of the damage came about at the hands of Cromwell's soldiers, who fought at the battle of St Fagans a few fields away in 1648. As I ruminate on the lives of these men I am reminded of the 'green' burial ground that caught my eye just outside Cardiff. There, the dead are laid to rest wrapped in a simple shroud, the spot marked by a freshly planted tree. This is burial as it once was for most people, simple and with little ceremony – all of which is great for the earth but bad for future curious church wanderers who linger beside a nice memorial.

long as the chores themselves. There is something approaching a military operation keeping this place going – I wonder what parish politics and village détente lurk between those lines of initials?

I try the church door's iron ring expecting it to be locked, but instead it swings open with a well-oiled clunk. Inside the cool, pale space is dominated by the scent of old candles in cold air and a dozen starlings singing above the choir. The straw dropped from the nest and flecks of bird mess on the wall seem oddly right and fitting. This is their home and I creep around feeling like an intruder. On the pews before the round stone font, a generous stack of second-hand paperbacks is for sale and beside them an honesty tin with a few pound coins left inside. To the side of the novels there are a dozen jars of apple chutney with pristine paper caps held by rubber bands turned twice round waiting to be taken away by a hungry visitor.

St Hilary of Poitiers was a fourth-century bishop. Few churches are named after him in Britain – perhaps unsurprisingly he is better known in France. The first records of St Hilary in Glamorgan date from 1116 but scholars think the church dates from pre-Norman times. The bulk of the present building – the nave, chancel, south aisle, south porch and west tower – dates from the late twelfth or early thirteenth century. The porch and aisle were added in the fourteenth century. However, much of what remains today was heavily restored in 1862 by the renowned Victorian architect Sir George Gilbert Scott.

Near the door beside a medieval holy water stoop, the visitor's book stands open on a lectern. I leaf through its awkward biro entries, which read like single-line family biographies. Some have returned here to remember weddings from decades ago, or perhaps retracing numbed steps after bereavement; others have been killing time here while visiting elderly loved ones at the nursing home across the road. Within these walls they've found distraction from awkward bedside small talk before returning to dutiful vigil.

St Hilary is a shrine to the changing fortunes of the wealthy families of the Vale of Glamorgan. Scott's restoration was paid for by Charlotte Traherne of Coedriglan in memory of her late husband, the Reverend John Montgomery Traherne. The decorative carving above the doorway includes three bugle horns, the arms of the Basset family of Beaupre Castle down the road.

Most of the windows date from Scott's restoration. The east window's depiction of the Passion, Crucifixion, Resurrection and Ascension was a gift from George Montgomery Traherne in memory of his sister. St Hilary is to be found in the west window of the south aisle. A depiction of the Last Supper, inspired by Leonardo da Vinci's masterpiece, is carved in marble on the wall beneath the east window. On a wall of the nave is a memorial to Daniel Jones of Beaupre who died in 1841. Jones was a wealthy lawyer and founder of the Cardiff Royal Infirmary. The memorial shows Jones's head encircled by a serpent devouring its tail, the ancient symbol of eternity that also reminds us of the snake of Asclepius, the Greek god of healing.

I close the porch door behind me and leave the visitor's book unsigned. The church is returned to the starlings and their choral evensong. Every time I walk into a church like this and find it open – its historical treasures on show for all to enjoy – my faith in humanity is restored.

I'm now having another quick wander around the village. The moss is getting a firm hold on the thatched roof of St Hilary's village pub – The Bush Inn is the beginning and the end of many Glamorgan walks. In the estate agent's local newspaper advertisment of the chocolate box cottage they have used an ancient black-and-white photograph of the property from about a century ago when it too had a thatched roof. A matronly occupant stands guard at the garden gate – I can't imagine that her hatched-faced stare is going to boost the prospects of sale.

Cowbridge High Street in about 1955 – it hasn't changed a great deal since.

Cowbridge

I think I've now seen all that St Hilary has to offer, so it's time for me to be heading over to my next destination: Cowbridge. It's just a few miles from here, through another kissing gate, over a farm track and across a paddock that stays stubbornly muddy even after days of baking sunshine. Then down a lane, along the track past the 'Private Road' sign and over the stile.

Cowbridge, the Vale's market town, is busy and affluent and seemingly unaffected by the haemorrhaging of business that other towns have suffered. Where so many Welsh high streets have been killed off by out-of-town developments, Cowbridge has refused to bend to the will of the large chains. Shopping and business are still done right in the centre here, as they have been for centuries. The bustling high street and narrow passages darting off it are lined with butchers, saddlers and land agents. As in that other splendid market town, Monmouth, the supermarkets here have been compelled to open up on the main street, within the premises of old buildings. In doing so, they contribute to the town's health rather than bleed it dry from the extremities. Bits of Tudor, Georgian and Victorian architecture sit side by side like mismatched crockery on an old Welsh dresser. Running behind the main street, overlooked by the ruins of the old town hall, the Physic Garden's quiet lawns, pond and trees offer a welcome oasis from the traffic.

When you wander around the streets this is one of those towns in Wales that 'feels right' – the town centre's businesses are still alive, people haven't abandoned living in its heart, and the new developments (which do not, I'm happy to see, break the tree line) have an empathy with their surroundings and a human scale. The handful of huge archways to the side of magnificent town houses once led to coaching stables – and where horses and hay were kept now boutiques and cafés watch over the cobbles. This is Wales at its poshest; the shoppers here this morning will mingle with some of the country's wealthiest people, footballers fleeing the city and media types secretly hoping to be recognized. The shops are a cut above your usual fare with designer clothes stores sitting next to delicatessens and countrywear stores. But amidst all the wealth, at the heart the town is a farming community that is in rude health.

The town hall is a former centre for correction – not that you sense that Cowbridge's leafy lanes would inspire much misbehaviour, it's not easy feeling violent or abusive when you're surrounded by trees. The three-storey townhouses are the work of the best stonemasons and their wealthy paymasters.

St Quentin's Castle

A short wander through the back roads of Cowbridge to the top of a loop in the River Thaw, St Quentin's Castle stands high on a hill and stares over the rooftops of the hamlet of Llanblethian. The ruin is now little more than a romantic tower, its days of striking fear into the hearts of the unruly long past. The distant traffic tearing down the tarmac on the bypass is an occasional reminder that the twenty-first century is never far away.

In about 1102 Robert Fitzhamon, the first Norman Lord of Glamorgan, granted the tiny Lordship of Llanblethian to Herbert de Quentin who, it is thought, may have established the first castle on this hill. Later in the twelfth century a rectangular stone keep was built. The Lordship remained in the hands of the St Quentin family until 1233 when it was seized by Richard Siward – who in turn lost it to Earl Richard de Clare in 1245.

Sometime after 1307, Richard's grandson Earl Gilbert de Clare began to build this present structure with its impressive gatehouse, much of which still stands to this day and is the substantial part of the ruin. The poor fellow was killed in the Battle of Bannockburn in 1314, before his fine home was completed. St Quentin's Castle continued to be lived in, half-finished, until the sixteenth century.

The gatehouse is now a hollow stone shell that looks gentle and modest in its decline; its immense thick walls contain a modern steel staircase and small viewing platforms. It's worth climbing to the top to see the rooftops of Llanblethian and the green fields beyond. Looking out at the distant horizon, I understand why the castle was built here – it's an ideal strategic position, perfect for watching people's movements for miles around.

Even in its ruined state, the gatehouse is still a substantial building, large enough to have proved a comfortable home. It compares well with those built by the Earl Gilbert's father up the road in Caerphilly and by Edward I at his forbidding castles in North Wales. The portcullis is long gone but the arrow slits to take out brave chancers still send a shiver down my spine.

The grounds behind the gatehouse have the appearance of a green tablecloth draped over an elephant; the green lawns hide an enormous pile of stones and embedded tree trunks, all as one now beneath the earth. It might be little more than a four-walled ruin but St Quentin's is a calming presence and a relic from Glamorgan's more dangerous times. One of the benches beneath the wall has been donated by the local WI; it's the perfect place to sit and watch the world go by.

In a cottage near the gatehouse a family discussion is taking place rather loudly in the garden late on a sunny afternoon. The climbing roses and the wall's wisteria hide the faces, but the gist is that Dad won't allow daughter to go out with her friends tonight – exam time is approaching and revision is required. A teenage stand-off takes place and St Quentin's still has one more mighty battle on its hands tonight.

Old Beaupre Castle

Once again I'm on the back roads, this time from Cowbridge to Old Beaupre Castle. From the top of the hill I can see the sea and, in the far distance, St Athan's enormous airliner servicing depot – its white hulk dwarfs every nearby barn and church. Beside it is Cardiff Airport, which we once called Rhoose before the age of nation building and branding. It's been renamed several times over the years – Rhoose Airport, Cardiff Airport, and now called Cardiff International Airport. Presumably at some point we will follow Liverpool John Lennon's example and rename it Cardiff Tom Jones or Cardiff Catherine Zeta-Jones. Highly skilled jobs at the airport pay for the upkeep of many a bucolic cottage around here, just a stone's throw from work. Beyond the huge hangar on a clear day the coastline of South-West England is just visible on the edge of the horizon. Cardiff is closer to England than it is to North and West Wales. We are a small country and yet so distant from each other.

Old Beaupre Castle is a distinguished ruin, still full of atmosphere.

The hedges and fields don't give up their secrets so easily in the summer. The rain and sun between them have lengthened branches and grass. The spreading green masks the past, but when the ground is parched and the grass turns yellow and brown you can look down and

pick out the line of the disused railway, its quiet bridges and overgrown track running past unconcerned cows.

At last I reach Old Beaupre Castle. Finding the entrance proves tricky – there's little in the way of signage, and the visitor car park is a modest lay-by at the side of a narrow road. I clamber over an old stone stile only to discover a plastic-sheathed sign tied to a post advising visitors that Cadw, the heritage board for Wales, has closed the ruin for essential repair work. So no exploring the interior today – the castle may only be enjoyed from the outside. Undeterred, I walk across a couple of fields to the ruin, which stands on a hill looking more like a manor house than a turreted castle. There's none of your usual tearooms or coach loads of tourists here. Instead, there are a few inquisitive cows waiting for teatime milking and a rather forlorn pile sitting in a lonely field, half-forgotten and distressed. There is, however, something romantic about the castle's decline and its isolation, and I can't help thinking that it would have ruined the atmosphere had they transformed Beaupre into some heritage theme park. The charm is its gentle decline sitting in the middle of the Welsh countryside and not much visited. Cadw's workmen will prevent a complete fall from grace but its ultimate fate will be paused rather than reversed.

I approach and try the gates but, true to their word, the stonemasons, archaeologists and conservators have barricaded the great planked doors. A scaffolding platform of rusting brown poles and dirty planks leans against the stonework. High winds give the insurers of the wobbly castle sleepless nights so the work aims to secure loose masonry. I can see a few yards of stone wall that has already had its joins scraped out and its crumbling cement replaced with lime mortar. You'd have to look closely to find the new work, it looks like the art of a talented forger – once the rain and the wind have done their best and blurred the joins. Confronted with so many centuries of decay, the workmen must wonder where to begin, but their task is to secure the walls and make them safe rather than restore the ruin.

In fact, considering how much this building has been fiddled about with over the years, with countless rebuildings and restylings, I wonder which age the restorers would even return it to. At its heart is an Elizabethan farmhouse, which is still in use and in private hands; the windowless ruins are later sixteenth-century additions. Among the few visitors to its gates are a growing number of film crews – most recently the producers of *Doctor Who* searching for a ghostly ancient house that had fallen on hard times. Nowhere else could play the part as perfectly as Old Beaupre Castle.

At least Old Beaupre has Cadw to act in its best interests; in a county full of farmsteads, castles and country houses, Glamorgan has more than its share of neglected ruins, many of which have little or no official protection. The future for so many of our old buildings in Wales lies in finding new uses for them that will help pay for their future without denigrating their past. Few owners can bear the weighty cost of renovation of large properties without making the building work for a living. I'll come back here when the restorers have finished and the scaffolding has been taken down and go inside that big brown door.

Plas Llanmihangel

Up the road from Old Beaupre Castle, through lanes too narrow for two passing cars, I come to the hamlet of Llanmihangel. It seems to consist of not much more than an ancient manor house – Plas Llanmihangel – overlooking a shaded church. Llanmihangel church sits at the bottom of the valley;

a few dozen stone steps take me from the lane to the churchyard gate. The porch door is situated on the sheltered side – the church is locked this afternoon but a friendly note invites callers to collect the key from the big house as an incentive for the doubly inquisitive. There's a fresh planter of primroses placed on one of the graves and someone has just left the churchyard after taking advantage of the drying sun to mow the grass. The heady summer mixture of two-stroke petrol and hot oil is still hanging thick in the air. A photographer wanders around outside the gate – he's been waiting for the sun to be directly overhead to best capture the light before the shadows from the trees cloak it in late afternoon shade. This is Glamorgan at its most achingly beautiful.

However, it's the manor house that I've really come to see. Plas Llanmihangel has been described by the Royal Commission on Ancient Monuments as one of the finest and most complete gentry houses in Glamorgan. It's also one of the best-kept secrets hereabouts – even many local people don't know about this place. The fortified manor stands on the slope of a gentle hill; built of the most wonderful limestone, it has a number of generous mullioned windows. The original estate would have covered about 400 acres, but the farm was separated from the house in the 1970s and the remaining 12 acres of land surrounding the house include a rare example of an untouched William and Mary garden, which has excited green-fingered historians. What is splendid about this place (apart from the fact that it is in such an excellent state of conservation) is that anyone can stay here – it's one of the country's best bed and breakfasts and at 33 quid a night possibly one of the best deals too.

The hamlet of Llanmihangel is described as being a 'grange' in 1166, at which point it was in the ownership of John Norreys, a Norman knight. The church is first mentioned in 1254 and historians are pretty sure that the manor house existed before then. The structure of the medieval house still stands, but in the sixteenth century some new owners gave it a makeover to bring it up to date with the latest look. Those new owners were the Thomas family who were connected to the Earls of Pembroke. After the sixteenth-century additions, not much was done to change the fabric of the building until the 1780s when the main bedroom was spruced up. The builders came back in the 1880s to bring the house up to the standards required of the late nineteenth century.

The result is a sprawling pile of gables, turrets, windows and chimneys. Its most remarkable architectural feature is the strikingly medieval first-floor hall, something that remained popular in Wales long after it fell from fashion elsewhere in Elizabethan times. At times of peril, Plas Llanmihangel's 12-foot-high stone walls on the south side, its defensible gatehouse and solid, windowless walls on the ground floor would have protected its cautious inhabitants from the worst of the prowling violence.

I decide to have a wander around the house. However well defended and fortified it appears from the outside, inside Plas Llanmihangel is every bit the comfortable gentry home. The oak-panelled hall with its decorative plasterwork is to this day the social hub for entertaining. The hall's large stone fireplace features the shields of the Thomas family and the De La Bere family – which, by coincidence, is also the name of the current owners, the Beers. This is a house capable of making you smile knowingly at history's little tricks.

Most charming of all, with every new door I open I discover a new chapter from history. Each room I enter reflects a different period in the eccentric building's long and varied past. The earliest sections of the house are almost monastic in their unadorned simplicity; others from later

Above: Plas Llanmihangel, a profusion of mullioned windows set in beautiful gardens.

Overleaf: The oak-panelled hall with its wonderful plasterwork ceiling and grand fireplace is the hub of Plas Llanmihangel.

PRESERVING THE PAST

So many historic houses in Britain are lost to public enjoyment either by dereliction or private ownership, while others can sometimes become preserved too perfectly so that the spirit leaves. At Plas Llanmihangel the essential qualities of a centuries-old home remain to be enjoyed by a wide audience and that is something to be cherished.

The manor's saviours David and Sue Beer have devoted their years to restoring a building that could have looked like nearby Old Beaupre Castle by now were it not for their tireless devotion. Their trick here has been to make the place work for its living and secure its own future. Rather than spending its years preserved in precarious aspic, eking out a living as a museum piece, Plas Llanmihangel is a living, working manor house earning its keep and ensuring its future.

You're as likely to stumble into a wedding or a birthday party if you call in at Plas Llanmihangel these days. In fact, however, it has always been at the centre of the community's life for celebration or gatherings of local import – as well as being used as a courtroom in the 1530s where the Lord of the Manor heard the parish's petty crimes.

centuries are sumptuous and gilded in their decoration. The stories of the people who have lived in Plas Llanmihangel are no less intriguing than the house. Sadly, the Thomas family who owned Plas Llanmihangel never really recovered from the costs of the Civil War and were not wealthy people. Sir Humphrey Edwin bought up all the Thomas's debts until he'd bankrupted them and got their home and lands at a fraction of the market price.

Great Frampton House

If Plas Llanmihangel is a textbook example of how to help a historic Glamorgan house survive, then Great Frampton House is its complete antithesis. Situated on the narrowest of back roads just before Llantwit Major, and dating from between the sixteenth and eighteenth centuries, Frampton at first sight looks like a building project abandoned a couple of centuries ago. Its roofless walls are optimistically propped up by scaffolding poles – it is as though the builders left the roofers to complete the job but they never came. On closer inspection this is a once grand house that was gutted by a merciless fire. Today its windows are gaping holes where the wood has been burnt from the stone. Peering over the front garden wall I see that the lawns are waist high in nettles – not even the black sheep grazing nearby will venture in.

If Great Frampton were just another historic house that had fallen on bad times, its decline would be sad but not unremarkable. What is particularly distressing about Frampton is that it has the kind of provenance that in England or the United States would have a trust fund endowed and an appeal to restore it. Frampton was the home of the renowned astronomer Nathaniel Piggot. He built an observatory in the grounds and his observations of the night sky were published by the Royal Society. It was sitting here looking up at the heavens in 1779 that he discovered a nebula in Coma Berenices. There's no blue plaque on the walls to commemorate his life. Perhaps it's just as well, since the walls probably couldn't take the weight.

As I look at the quiet, empty barns and garden I imagine old Mr Board, a gardener from Devon who walked to Wales with only a shilling in his pocket to begin a new life here. He became bailiff initially and then took on the tenancy of the estate. His son was famed in the 1930s for breeding Aberdeen Angus and Dairy Shorthorn cows. In those days Frampton picked up many of the country's agricultural rosettes which might, after a hearty celebration on coming home, have been pinned up on the back one of those rotting barn doors now swinging in the breeze.

Sadly, Frampton won't be on many tourist itineraries. It certainly isn't featured in many guidebooks to Wales, but to my mind understanding a country is as much about looking for what we do not want to feature. When Frampton has fallen down we will lament its passing and express regret that a chapter of our history has slipped into rubble.

 *Llantwit Major*

It's day two of my wanders around the Vale of Glamorgan and early in the morning in St Illtud's churchyard. The church dominates Llantwit Major's history and the story of religious life of South Wales. This little community is home to one of the oldest Christian sites in the United Kingdom – for more than 1500 years the faithful have worshipped at this beautiful spot in the middle of the Vale of Glamorgan. Illtud came

The Old Swan Inn in Llantwit Major, a charming pub in one of Wales's most important religious sites.

The church of St Illtud in Llantwit Major, originally founded by the hermit saint in the sixth century.

here in AD 500 and though little is known about him, much is known about his church. The porch welcomes parishioners where the original Celtic church stood.

At the far end of the church the ladies of Llantwit are cleaning the silverware behind the huge curtain in a corner. They don't hear the heavy metallic clunk of the turning of the door handle – they are too deep in conversation and occasional song. Here the tea and biscuits, cups and saucers, sit in disciplined order beside the boiler. The vacuum cleaner and the dusters too are screened off from view. Every so often during a lull in their cleaning conversation one of the ladies bursts into an unconscious rendition of a favourite hymn: 'All things bright and beautiful, All creatures great and small... All things wise and wonderful, the Lord God made them all...'. At the end of every other line the singer stops, as if interrupted or simply unable to recall the rest of the verse. 'Dear Lord and Father of mankind, forgive our foolish ways...' – and then the sound of polish squirting from an aerosol as the ancient silverware is rubbed to within an inch of

BRITAIN'S OLDEST SCHOOL

*Christianity was first brought to the British Isles by the Romans. When they departed the religion declined in England but survived in the further flung corners of coastal Britain – particularly in Wales and Cornwall. Christianity's survival and revival was inspired by Celtic saints, holy men who wandered these lands preaching and establishing religious communities. Illtud, one of these holy men, came to Llantwit as a hermit but ended up establishing a church, a school and a monastery here. What little we know of Illtud comes from a book about Samson, one of Illtud's pupils. In **The Life of St Samson** Illtud is described as a Breton and 'the most learned of all Britons in scripture, philosophy, poetry, rhetoric, grammar and arithmetic. He was gifted with the power of foretelling events.'*

Samson wasn't the only distinguished scholar to study here at Llantwit. Gildas, the author of the first book on Welsh history, studied here before going on to found the monastery at Rouel in Brittany and the cathedral at Dol, near St Malo. Another Llantwit scholar, Paul Aurelian, built his monastery at St Paul de Leon.

*Llantwit Major was one of only three religious centres in Britain that practised **laus perennis** or 'unceasing praise'. The students were divided up into 24 groups and each given responsibility for one hour of worship, so that prayer and praise were offered continually to God. (If you're interested, the other two religious centres were to be found at Old Sarum and Glastonbury.)*

*The **Guinness Book of Records** lists Llantwit as the site of Britain's oldest seat of learning. Nothing remains of the original fifth-century buildings, and the nature of the school is open to conjecture – was it a university or something smaller? The Welsh revisionist Iolo Morganwg may have stretched the truth when he inflated Llantwit's classes to 'seven churches with seven colleges and two thousand students', but the importance of Llantwit Major as a school and a monastery is unquestionable. Hundreds of years before Oxford and Cambridge were turning out scholars, in this quiet corner of the Vale of Glamorgan, Llantwit Major was home to a substantial seat of learning.*

obscurity. How these ancient places of worship in Wales would decline were it not for the unceasing industry of the army of volunteers who cheerfully work tirelessly week in, week out. Their sporadic and random verses are the accompaniment to the rest of my visit.

The walls are mostly whitewashed except for the breathtaking friezes high up on the wall near the roof. They give an inkling of the riot of colour and decoration that would have covered this church before religion took a turn towards the austere and its paintings were covered over with hundreds of years of white paint. It is in these faded figures and their now drab clothes that Llantwit's long history reaches out from the walls.

Anglesey

MENAI STRAIT ◉ LLANFAIR PG ◉ PLAS NEWYDD ◉
MARQUESS OF ANGLESEY'S COLUMN ◉ BEAUMARIS
CASTLE

'M STANDING in Cardiff International Airport, staring at the departures
board. All the familiar holiday destinations are displayed: Malaga,
Paris, Dublin, all beckoning a new crowd of holidaymakers. Finally
I spot my flight: HWY 0601 Highland Airways for... Anglesey.

You can spot the passengers for Anglesey: we have less luggage than
the passengers flying to the sun, and instead of shorts and T-shirts we're
wearing waterproofs and walking boots. Neither do we need passports
at check-in – all that is required is photographic identification and an
email ticket confirmation. My plan is to explore Anglesey and
Snowdonia, and then – weather permitting – climb Snowdon.

*OPPOSITE: The unforgettable
coastline of Anglesey by
South Stack, an unspoilt
haven for walkers and
birdwatchers.*

◉

This was the first airport I flew from. It was a school exchange to Brittany when I was 13.
François Xavier came to Pembrokeshire for a few weeks to stay with us, and later in the year I
went to stay with his family in La Boule. I flew from here on my own – my first ever flight all by
myself seemed very glamorous at the time. I learnt very little French from the experience, but
François Xavier learnt the full canon of English swearwords from my brother Huw, which I'm sure
impressed his parents when he returned home to France.

The Highland Airways service departs at 07:30 and arrives at the RAF Valley base on Anglesey at
08:35. This is a relatively new service, and is subsidized by the Welsh Assembly Government. Its
creation was deeply controversial, with critics pointing out that air travel isn't environmentally
friendly and that if there was taxpayer's money available to subsidize travel, then why not invest it
in railways or roads. The fact is that the air service is the result of a political decision to try to bring
together a far-flung country (though since it only carries 19 passengers at a time, it may take a while
to bring all three million of us together). There's talk that the air service might be expanded to other
routes and to a weekend operation – at the moment this is strictly a Monday to Friday arrangement.

The BAE Jetstream 31 Turboprop sitting right outside the terminal building looks more like a
large people carrier than a commercial aircraft. There's just one short ladder leading up to the
passenger cabin. The plane's name is painted on the side: 'Gogledd a De', Welsh for 'North and

South', and just for good measure there's a red dragon in flight on the side of its nose cone. The lady at the check-in desk says they've carried more passengers in the first two years of operation than they tendered for in their three-year contract. Critics had suggested that this would be a taxpayer-funded service that would only be used by civil servants, but the airline staff say this isn't the case.

It's drizzling gently as we walk from Gate Eight across the tarmac to the back of the plane. Among my fellow travellers are the Welsh Assembly Government's Health Minister Edwina Hart and her special advisor Jo Kiernan, both heading for the National Eisteddfod taking place at Bala where the Minister will be on duty. Last week I kept her waiting in the rain to do an interview about swine flu; we had a technical problem that took a while to be resolved. She was very polite about it, although it meant she looked like a drowned rat when we got round to filming. I'm hoping she's forgotten. The other passengers are largely men who look business-like with technical magazines, laptops and beards. It's a tight squeeze to get into the cabin, the headroom is limited and there isn't much room in the aisle either. There are seven empty seats so most of us have room to spread out.

Once we are seated and buckled, the captain turns around in the cockpit and stands up to begin the safety briefing. 'Sharon is on her holidays this week,' he explains to the regulars – who are presumably concerned about the absence of a familiar face – before proceeding to demonstrate the life jackets and exits. It's more difficult to carry on reading the paper during such a personal address and he has everyone's attention.

We're so close to the cockpit that we can hear at least one side of the radio discussion with the control tower, but as soon as the screaming engines accelerate, any conversation or the ability to listen to one comes to an end. This is noisy – very noisy. Taxiing past the other aircraft waiting for departure this plane feels like a gnat buzzing at the hides of lumbering elephants. The noise and speed increase until we've got enough momentum to catapult off the tarmac. I notice each of us has not one but two sick bags protruding from the pouch in front of us. As they say in flying circles: small aircraft – big vomit.

Houses and cars get smaller below us and, like a toddler pulling itself to its feet, the little aircraft twitches and turns for a few moments before reaching up steeply and steadying into its climb. The Bristol Channel is flat calm this morning and the sun kisses the water around Flat Holm Island off the coast of Cardiff. We fly over the sea towards England for a few moments in what seems to be the wrong direction and then bank steeply left and head northeast, following the tightly controlled air corridors of the busy passenger airport and its neighbour, RAF St Athan.

I look out of the window. Unrolling beneath us are the posh sea-facing terraces of Penarth and the tree-lined streets of Cardiff cut in half by the River Taff. A minute or two later we are flying over the flat patchwork fields of the Vale of Glamorgan, the brown, yellow and green squares disappearing momentarily behind wisps of grey cloud.

Above the clouds, above the mountains and moody rain, the sun always shines and the sky is always bright blue – if only Wales had been built a few thousand feet higher. Our route today will take us in a straight line from Cardiff to Anglesey, although this isn't always the case on this flight; our destination airport is shared with RAF Valley, so the civilian service has to vary its route depending on the activities of the pilot flying school there. If the student pilots (who this year include Prince William) are at large then the passenger service gives them a wide berth and takes a rectangular route above Offa's Dyke on the English border and then turns left along the North Wales coast.

Even when viewed from the sky, Wales is a difficult country to consider as a whole. We are perhaps more loyal to our counties and to our cities than to any notion of 'country' – except,

THE WELSH DIASPORA

Transport has certainly shaped Wales's history. Far-flung communities of the west coast such as Aberystwyth and Aberaeron were once located on the motorway of life when travel by water was king. Before air transport Wales was at the heart of world trading routes and its people were the captains, crew and traders travelling the globe and building their fine houses on the coast with the proceeds. Travel to the Caribbean and look at the names of the villages and ask the surnames of the locals and you will find surnames like Jones living in places called Pembroke (and even the occasional story of double lives and double families).

You don't hear much about the story of the Welsh Diaspora – not in comparison to Ireland's and Scotland's tales – but it is a considerable and rich story. As a people we are good mixers, we quickly become part of new countries. We are slow to burden others with our past and our culture so we assimilate quickly into the Australias and Americas, often losing our distinctive identity (although in certain parts of Argentina there are still Welsh-speaking communities). Unlike our Celtic cousins whose projected identity is kept alive in the world's Irish-themed pubs, the Welsh could never be associated with anything so publicly sinful. After all, this is a country where you would struggle to get a drink on a Sunday until a few years ago.

perhaps, in matters of rugby or where any dispute with England is concerned. (You only have to meet football supporters of Cardiff or Swansea to understand that loyalty to city is all.) Both devolution referendums exposed the fact that we are a divided country. We are divided in our politics and our ambitions for the future of Wales, and that in no small part is because of how distant we are from each other. Quite simply the geography makes Wales a collection of isolated tribes. The roads run largely from east to west along the coastal corridors, while the valleys run north to south. Throw in the odd mountain range like the Brecon Beacons (far beneath us right now), and you can see what I mean.

There's no in-flight breakfast – the journey is too short and the plane too small – but coffee and biscuits are served by the stand-in flight attendant who can't stand up straight in the aisle because he is too tall. The curtain that separates the captain from the passengers doesn't stop the sound of the altitude alarm or a flurry of radio messages about wind direction and airstrip activity.

The thwack of the undercarriage dropping means we are a short distance away from RAF Valley. After 35 minutes in the air we are descending from the clouds and dropping towards the long arm of the Llyn Peninsula pointing out to sea. Wales is still grey and damp as we descend from the clouds. Back on earth it is still a cloudy, misty and cool August day – even if we are now in North Wales.

Looking out I can see Snowdon glowering in the mist – even at this distance its convection currents are buffeting our descent. The plane feels its way down from the heights pitching and rocking, like a climber moving down a mountain on gravel. Anglesey's roads beneath us are still quiet enough for us to land on should the need arise. We circle the island, bank steeply and are now low enough to see the faces of dog walkers throwing sticks on the beach.

OVERLEAF: *The elegant Menai Bridge finally connected Anglesey to the mainland in 1826. Before then, the island could only be reached by boat.*

Arriving in Anglesey

The island of Anglesey was once a formidable destination, surrounded on all sides by sea, with ferocious tides and currents keeping guard over the Menai Strait. These days it is permanently connected to the mainland by road and railway bridges – but never suggest to anyone here that it is no longer an island. I've sailed around Anglesey a few times – its coastline is the most delightful mix of dramatic cliffs and lighthouses and challenging navigation up the Menai Strait, but I readily admit to not having explored much of the island itself.

Celtic Britain was run from Anglesey for many years. The tiny fishing village of Aberffraw, just visible now through the plane window, was the ancient capital of the kings of Gwynedd. There's little left to tell of the royal court that was once here, but at one time this was a thriving centre of patronage and government. Below us now is the tiny church of St Cwyfan's, built on an island just off the shore. Accessible only at low tide (with the risk of wet feet), it dates from 605 and looks as magical from the air as it does from the water.

The Welsh name for Anglesey is Ynys Môn – Ynys in Welsh means 'island' and Môn stems from a Celtic word for 'end'. It is also known as Mam Cymru – 'mother of Wales' – a name arising from the island's extensive cornfields. It was what lay below the earth, however, that gave Anglesey its big break: this was the world's copper capital. Copper was mined here 4,000 years ago and throughout Parys Mountain's working life the trade in this metal paid for many of the grand houses and great estates on the island.

Anglesey was also the heartland of the druids, who were attacked by the Roman Suetonius Paulinus and virtually eliminated by his successor Agricola. Their martyrdom ensured that they passed into Welsh mythology. Tacitus records that 'Natives smeared their altars with blood from their prisoners and sought the will of the gods by exploring the entrails of men.' The princes of Gwynedd chose Anglesey as their stronghold – and it wasn't a bad choice, since the island endured generations of raids from the Norsemen. That long tradition of feeling under pressure from authorities far away looks set to continue – this week's local newspaper reports that the Welsh Assembly Government is sending in its own senator to take control of Anglesey council's affairs after condemnation of its administration from the auditor general. Let's hope he doesn't get the entrail treatment.

We are close enough to the sand now to be able to land on the beach but the long, purpose-built airstrip is just coming into view. After 42 minutes of flying across Wales we touch down at RAF Valley – 15 minutes ahead of schedule. It's a slightly unnerving experience taxiing along the tarmac surrounded by dozens of BAE Hawk TMK 1 jets, their lights flashing and their ground crews moving clear. Like angry wasps caught in a jar, they are impatient to get back into the air. The pilots watch us from their glass domes; they will take a matter of minutes to cover the journey that has taken us nearly three quarters of an hour. Their flight will skim over mountains and telegraph poles, and drop low over the lakes. For training purposes the Welsh countryside will play the part of Afghanistan – except here there'll be no firing of missiles from the ground. I keep an eye out for the Prince, but they all look the same in their helmets and flying suits.

There's no customs to clear at Anglesey, so we clamber out of the back of the cabin and walk to the brand new (and tiny) arrivals and departures terminal. A small band of passengers is gathered to make the return journey to Cardiff. There are a dozen or so plastic seats in the waiting area, no shop, and the monitor offers only one destination now the gate has closed for the return flight – Cardiff at 16:15. After my fellow travellers have gone on their way I'm the only one left in the terminal apart from the cleaning staff. Since the bus is tied to the scheduled landing time, I've got half an hour to kill. At least there's a shelter from the drizzle.

Most people in Wales know Valley for its military air training work, but long before the MoD came here in 1941 Thomas Telford is thought to have given the place its name when he built his road through here. Millennia before Telford it was home to Iron Age man, whose pots, pans and farming implements, all unearthed within a few yards of me, are now on display at the National Museum of Wales in Cardiff.

Like Pembrokeshire, Anglesey is home to a port onto the Irish Sea, at Holyhead. This port is the reason why the bridges to the mainland and the straight main roads were built – to move mail, goods and passengers swiftly across the Irish Sea. Like Pembroke Dock and Fishguard in the south of the country, however, this means that Anglesey is seen as a conduit to get somewhere else, rather than as a destination in its own right – which, from what I've seen, strikes me as a shame.

 *Anglesey by Bus*

The Menai Bridge has always been a tight squeeze for buses!

It's £3 for a single ticket to Menai Bridge. The bus turns up on time with six other passengers already collected on its drive from further up the island. There couldn't be a more roundabout way of exploring anywhere than by taking the bus. In a car this drive would take me no more than ten minutes, but slowly weaving in and out of every village and hamlet will give me a taste of the B-roads.

From Valley we drive across the A55 dual carriageway and pick up the back roads to Bryngwyn, to Gwalchmai, Bodffordd, turn right to Llangefni and Pentre Berw. And, of course, the famous village of Llanfair PG – or, to give it its full name,

LLANFAIRPWLLGWYNGYLLGOGERYCHWYRNDROBWLLLLANTYSILIOGOGOGOCH
(*'St Mary's Church in a hollow by the white hazel close to the rapid whirlpool by the red cave of St Tysilio'*).

Cynics will remind you that the name was dreamt up in the nineteenth century in a deliberate attempt to encourage tourism.

LLANFAIRPWLLGWYNGYLLGOGERYCHWYRNDROBWLLLLANTYSILIOGOGOGOCH

Llan-vire-pooll-guin-gill-go-ger-u-queern-drob-ooll-llandus-ilio-gogo-goch

Way Out ←

Holyhead →

They've been busy on the farms this weekend, and the hay has been rolled up ready for its black plastic wrap. The villages we are travelling through would once have been clogged with countless cars and lorries making their way to the Holyhead ferry, but a new, faster road has spared them this. Looking at them as we pass it also strikes me that they may have lost some of their life-blood, too. We stop to let a middle-aged man get off. He knows the driver and they say they'll see each other again tomorrow.

You can't visit Anglesey without taking a photo of Britain's longest railway station sign!

On the A5 to Gwalchmai we turn off to Gwalchmai Uchaf by the war memorial. Two ladies with walking sticks lumber on board and sit heavily; they shout in Welsh to confirm that they are safely in their seats, like ageing dowagers addressing their chauffeur. We turn left at Mona Industrial Park and pass another airfield; this is Bodffordd and for a moment the sun comes out to spotlight Snowdon across the fields on the mainland, sitting beneath a crown of cloud.

An old lady with empty shopping bags and a teenager get off at Llangefni. The streets are already bustling and half a dozen passengers get on. Some of them know each other and lean over the seats to exchange gossip; a gummy old man tells an acquaintance behind him that he's off to the dentist in Menai Bridge and he opens his mouth wide to show his collection of decayed yellowing pegs. We take off for Gaerwen with a lurch; the bus's automatic gearbox is jerky and juddery. A horsebox full of bleating lambs for market slows us down at Pentre Berw, and then we turn off to Llanddaniel past the Gaerwen Arms as the sun makes another, longer and more promising appearance to watch our criss-crossing every hamlet between Valley and Menai Bridge.

There are now 14 passengers aboard. A young couple dressed in business suits, perhaps colleagues or lovers, talk animatedly to each other throughout their journey, blissfully unaware of the presence of anyone else. A scruffy man who got on board with a wheeled shopping basket pulls faces at himself in the window. The blonde teenage girl on the seat to my side fiddles with her iPod and an annoying metallic, rhythmic tink tink comes out of its earphones, too quiet to discern the tune (if there is one). At Llanfair PG, the spiritual home of Britain's Women's Institute (which was founded here in 1915), a well-dressed lady in wide blue hat and sunglasses gets on, replacing the bloke in a T-shirt and moustache who looked as though he were ex-military. The town with the longest name in the world is twinned with the Dutch town of d'Ee.

For a small island you could spend a month travelling around this flat countryside and never scratch the surface of Anglesey. Naturalists come to walk the coast and watch the spectacular sea bird colonies at South Stack; in an ancient land with a greater concentration of prehistoric remains than anywhere else in the country, archaeologists pore over prehistoric life when druids and Romans walked the earth, and sailors love the challenging waters that switch between shelter and storm. But my interests on this trip lie on the eastern coast at Plas Newydd – the ancestral home of the Marquesses of Anglesey and, further up the road, the world heritage site of Beaumaris, home to a castle of almost perfect symmetry.

The remote South Stack lighthouse on the northwest coast of Anglesey was built to protect ships sailing from Holyhead to Dublin.

 Plas Newydd

The National Trust property of Plas Newydd sits in some of the most splendid gardens in Anglesey.

'Menai Bridge!' shouts the driver. Just as well he does – I'd have missed my stop. I could catch another bus from here, but a taxi rank temptingly nearby is too much to resist for the short hop to Plas Newydd – and in any case my rucksack is too heavy to walk comfortably.

Dave, my taxi driver, complains about the many speed cameras in North Wales – the UK's low-speed capital. He says it's an occupational hazard and hopes the retirement of the local Chief Constable may see them reduced. Since I'm keen to spend some time at Plas Newydd wandering around the house and gardens, he offers to drop me off, look after my rucksack and come back later. I've never met him before but something about Dave has me handing over my rucksack containing my laptop computer and all my worldly goods (well a few pairs of clean pants anyway).

There's already a small gathering outside the National Trust's ticket office. The entrance gates don't open until midday (by which time Dave's taximeter would have exploded), but the good news is that there's going to be a special tour behind the scenes for the early birds waiting at the gates and it begins in ten minutes. Perfect.

Walking down the hill through the grounds, past the avenue of trees that form an honour guard, I think to myself that there probably couldn't be a better place to build a stately home (and believe me I have given this a great deal of thought). The three-storey eighteenth-century house was designed by the fashionable architect James Wyatt and sits on the side of the Menai Strait with its back to Anglesey and looking across to Snowdonia. Its view of the mountains and forests would make a great painting, with yachts in full sail adding a dash of garish red and yellow foreground detail. The house in a grey render isn't conventionally beautiful or even grand, but in its veil of creepers it is both striking and understated.

A sudden shower scatters the group as we scurry under the generous canopies of trees. The doors to Plas Newydd open promptly at 11:15 to us chosen few and we are faced with a lady of advancing years with her spectacles on a chain. She greets her early birds (who number just five) as though we were her houseguests for the weekend. She is a volunteer and, judging by her beautiful accented English, originally from France. She leads the way into the house and motions to some chairs. This must be one of those few occasions in a National Trust house when visitors are invited to sit down without fear of an attendant swooping to preserve the nation's treasured possessions.

'Let's start in Lady Anglesey's Bedroom,' invites our guide, bidding her charges to follow her up the stairs. It's not clear whether the good Lady Anglesey will be propped up on her pillows waiting for us, but we march on obediently and mute.

The main staircase is a magnificent piece of joinery. The man in front of me, from Birmingham, obviously knows about carpentry, and caresses the turned spindles, huge newel post and everlasting handrail. His wife whispers loudly not to touch anything in case he breaks it. Our upward mobility is viewed suspiciously at all times by the family portraits staring down from the walls. The 1st Marquess of Anglesey commissioned John Lucas in 1840 to paint a portrait of the Duke of Wellington that hangs here. Wellington wrote to the artist that he 'was much flattered by Anglesey's desire to possess a portrait of me…I beg you to recollect…how desirable it is to attend to the size of the head…the head of those you have painted even that in the robes of the Chancellor of Oxford is too large; I always thought so; and you may rely upon it that I am right'.

Lady Anglesey's Bedroom is rather dark; the blinds and curtains are still drawn in late morning, not to save the slumbering incumbent but to keep out the daylight and its damaging rays. As my

TURNING BACK TIME

The Welsh climate makes the work of the National Trust and similar organizations more than difficult. On our tour of the house the guide takes pains to point out the challenges that they face. The damp, the wind, the rain and occasionally even the sun play havoc with the fabric, so the house's atmosphere is heavily controlled with year-round heating at a constant temperature still provided by the original boiler fitted generations ago.

In the bedroom our guide hands round two light bulbs for us to examine, a conventional bulb and a new low-energy fitting. She explains that the original chandeliers of the house had been converted from candle to electric without problems, but that the newer bulbs were so heavy that their weight would bring down the ceilings. This is the sort of everyday conundrum that is faced when running a National Trust home – balancing the need to do the right thing with a respect for the integrity of the property.

Sunlight is perhaps the least expected problem. All of the windows in Plas Newydd have been covered in a special film that reduces the amount of UV light entering the rooms, and the blinds and curtains are closed for much of the day. This is to prevent the fabric from discolouring. Our guide also shows us the light and water meters used to measure the levels in each room. The campaign to keep Plas Newydd firmly in the 1930s uses every tool at its disposal.

eyes adjust I see that it is an enormous room, a bedroom combined with sitting room, a chaise at the end of the bed for those moments when either a bed or a chair just won't do; a heart-shaped dressing table festooned with baubles and potions is reflected in the mirror.

The good lady is not in residence here and has not been for many a long year. The Angleseys still live in Plas Newydd, but since the National Trust has taken over the management of the house they live in private quarters away from the public rooms. Not that you'd guess: the whole house has the atmosphere of being lived in.

After seeing another couple of rooms and hearing more about the conservation work being carried out here we all obediently retrace our steps down to the stairs to Gothick Hall, where the house is formally open. Most of us decide to take a tour of the rest of the property but this time without a guide.

It's Barbara, another volunteer, who's holding the fort at the entrance this time. Barbara invites the growing number of punters gathering at the enormous front door to leave large bags with her in case they knock over something priceless and forbids us to take any photographs too (presumably the National Trust's light meter would self-destruct if exposed to a camera flash).

The Music Room is the first room on the ground floor tour, unless you disobey the feisty Barbara's instructions and walk in the opposite direction, something I would not recommend. It's in this room that 13-year-old Princess Victoria recorded her stay here in her journal: she 'danced the galop' in October 1832, she wrote, and 'stayed up till near nine'. Boy, that girl knew how to party.

Any performance, dancing or otherwise, is strictly discouraged these days; a sign on the grand piano says: DO NOT PLAY THE GRAND PIANO. I wonder if they'd object if Mozart popped in and tinkled the ivories. A furtive look towards Barbara in the doorway suggests that amending the sign to DO NOT PLAY THE GRAND PIANO...BADLY would be ill advised.

Lord Anglesey's Bedroom is just opposite his wife's. There's a tweed sports jacket slung over his desk chair as though he were about to pop back and continue writing his letters. The bed and wardrobe are enormous, and through a door in the corner of the bedroom lies the key to every long and happy relationship – not just separate bedrooms but a separate bathroom too.

Downstairs in the Octagon Room, the house is filling up with a healthy number of visitors including a father pointing out the wooden spinning globe to his teenage children. He tells them about Peter Sellers playing Inspector Clouseau in the film *The Pink Panther* and the scene where the famous detective spins the globe with his fingers but then forgets that he has put the antique in motion when he absent-mindedly leans against it only to lose his balance and fall over. The father is reduced to hysterics in retelling the tale – his children have never heard of Peter Sellers, Clouseau or the Pink Panther and edge away embarrassed as he dabs his cheeks.

For all the delights of nosing around the public rooms at Plas Newydd, it is Rex Whistler's giant mural in the Dining Room that stops most visitors in their tracks. The mural depicts a fantastical view inspired from locations experienced by the Angleseys and Whistler. The town on the mural and its architecture is a compilation of domes, spires and columns inspired by Italy, Germany, London and Austria nuzzling beside Snowdonia's mountains, Bangor's waterfalls and Caernarfon's castle. There's even a place for Whistler's much-loved Brighton. It's a piece of artistic entertainment with no deeper meaning; its colours are light and put a smile on your face.

The mural contains two figures commonly accepted to be Romeo and Juliet. A girl leans out of the window while a young man leans on the wall gazing up at her. It's thought that there is a strong possibility that these figures represent Whistler and Caroline, the daughter of the

Angleseys, whom Whistler painted frequently. Whistler was known to be in love with Caroline, though this was not reciprocated. Whistler later wrote to Lord Anglesey on settlement of his account: 'I could never hope to repay for all those lovely days of fun, sunshine, bathing, luxurious nights and enormous meals.' You can't help thinking that his time at Plas Newydd with the family meant so much more to Whistler than the commission's artistic and pecuniary value.

The mural at Plas Newydd by the gifted young artist Rex Whistler.

The Angleseys appear elsewhere on the canvas – beside the closed church doors, for example, stands one of the family who was notorious for always arriving late so that he might avoid the service. Two of the family's dogs that kept Whistler company while he worked sit on the steps of one panel; and so too do Lady Anglesey's spectacles, which Whistler painted in so that she would always have a pair handy. A lit cigarette sits on the step, its smoke curling upwards as it waits for Whistler to return to finish it.

The 58-foot-long mural was painted on a single canvas specially woven in France. The work was transported to Plas Newydd partly painted and stuck to the wall with glue; when bubbles appeared on the surface they did as every self-respecting decorator would do – got the iron out and flattened the offending bumps.

The artist Whistler was a great friend of the Anglesey family. Theirs was a relationship beyond client and contractor and they were among his greatest patrons. Whistler's Arcadian style found favour in Britain with a generation who had witnessed the horror and grief of the First World War. His talent stretched to book illustration, theatre design for John Gielgud, as well as opera, ballet and film work while also, when time permitted, painting murals for the aristocracy of North Wales.

The last of Whistler's letters to Plas Newydd, written in 1940, explains his reasons for joining the Welsh Guards: 'I've tried repeatedly in vain to get some use out of my drawing. I expect I've been an awful fool, but I had to make my mind up once and quickly. Longing to come up to Plas Newydd, and swear that I will dot the Anchors and cross the Masts then.' He never did come back. His life was cut tragically short in 1944 by an enemy mortar while he was clearing the tracks of a tank. Here he lives forever, marvelled over and revered.

The final rooms on the extensive tour are the smaller former domestic offices, now given over to a permanent exhibition of the relics and portraits of the 1st Marquess and his part in the Battle of Waterloo. It was his heroics in that conflict that saw the 2nd Lord of Uxbridge created 1st Marquess of Anglesey – though his celebrated elopement with Wellington's sister-in-law probably wasn't a great boost for the esprit de corps.

Towards the end of the battle his leg was smashed by grapeshot, upon which Uxbridge declared to Wellington: 'By God, sir, I've lost my leg!' – to which Wellington, momentarily removing his field glass and glancing down, replied: 'By God, sir, so you have!' On Uxbridge's return to London, the Prince Regent declared that he loved him and that he was 'his best officer and his best subject' – which must have made Wellington spit.

The town of Waterloo commemorated the loss of the now-celebrated limb by commissioning a unique monument that stands (as it were) to this day. Back at Plas Newydd, the 1st Marquess was clearly not a man to be held back by such a trifle, and set about finding a replacement limb. The Anglesey leg, as used by the Marquess, must count as one of the more peculiar exhibits to be found behind the glass of an exhibition case. It was patented by James Potts of Northumberland and was the world's first articulated wooden leg. Perhaps more peculiar still, you can also see a sprig of willow from the tree in whose shade the original limb was buried (with full military honours), and the leather stump cap worn subsequently by Lord Anglesey. Happily the 1st Marquess went on to hold some of the highest offices in the land, fathered 18 children and died at the grand old age of 84.

The Gardens of Plas Newydd

I leave the house and enter the grounds of Plas Newydd, which are bathed in sunshine. On the lawns running down to the water's edge three toddlers run after each other a little unsteadily – they squeal with delight, celebrating their seemingly boundless freedom in the great outdoors. Further up the bank, four families are sitting on their rugs picnicking on the grass. The Owen family would never have been let loose near a National Trust property at such a young age – our misbehaviour would have frazzled the nerves of parents and staff alike. But the Trust has loosened its stays from those starchy years and it's wonderful to see so many young people chasing around the grounds. If places like this are to have any hope of a long-term future it is with this new generation of visitors who will grow up loving the houses and gardens as much as their parents do. A huge spreading chestnut tree is being scaled by two older boys, who are utterly entranced – they will never forget this holiday in North Wales. Days out like this should be offered on prescription to our increasingly depressed, cooped-up urban population. There is nothing quite so good for your soul as sitting under trees watching the boats go by.

The grounds are looked after by four full-time gardeners bolstered by an army of volunteers. Happily the gardens are shielded from the worst of the Welsh winds.

The arboretum in particular is breathtaking. Its lofty specimens of Blue Atlantic Cedar, azaleas, Japanese Maples and cherries are beautifully set off by the massed pink, blue and purple rhododendrons, all at their best this week. A Middle Eastern family wander though the grounds past eucalyptus and southern beech, delighted and surprised at this sunny afternoon in Wales. The gardens have suffered some losses of taller specimens through gales, age and disease; but in their absence the sun penetrates and new growth flourishes.

Two gardeners hoe at a border of rhododendrons – there are five acres of then – filling up their trailer with weeds, cuttings and dead wood. It's a seemingly endless task but not without

The gardens at Plas Newydd are the ideal place to find a bit of peace and quiet.

its reward. Finishing one patch, they move on to a border the size of a cricket pitch and begin all over again.

The reliability of Welsh rain and the house's position so close to the sea have made the grounds at Plas Newydd an ideal habitat for exotic specimens from all corners of the earth. The great landscape gardener Humphry Repton came here in 1799 and wrote a rather sniffy report about what he saw: 'they have proceeded too hastily in grubbing hedges and pulling down cottages, for the sake of clearing an extent of open lawn in a direction where plantations ought to be encouraged to screen a bleak country.' Even then they suffered the curse of the Alan Titchmarsh instant garden – at least there's no decking.

The first Marquess planted a great number of trees after 1815 but this marked the beginning of a period of decline for both the house and garden. An account of the house in 1845 tells of the 'entire neglect into which it has fallen for more than twenty years'.

The whole estate was nearly lost at the hands of the 5th Marquess (the 'Dancing Marquess' as he was known). He lost his mother at the age of two and was brought up in France. From an early age he was fascinated by the theatre and in 1901, supported by the leading lights from the London stage, founded his own company. He staged lavish productions at Plas Newydd in the theatre (which had been converted from the chapel). He toured the provincial theatres of Britain and his 'Butterfly Dance' went down a storm in Berlin, with the proceeds being donated to local charities. His taste for the theatrical extended to life off stage and to his home and gardens at Plas Menai. He had braziers kept alight in the grounds in winter in case he became cold while walking outdoors. Though exceedingly wealthy, the 5th Marquess's passion for the good life, expensive cars, lavish jewellery and the best clothes eventually caught up with him. The newspapers dubbed his fall 'the great Anglesey sales'. It took 40 days to sell 17,000 lots at auction ranging from cars to pets. He died the following year, just short of his thirtieth birthday.

Marquess of Anglesey's Column

The column was erected to commemorate a hero of the Battle of Waterloo.

A little way up the road from the entrance to Plas Newydd, four ponies lie fast asleep in a field. They look like they're dead until my distant footsteps on the loose gravel first stir and then startle them. Just above them is a path that leads to the Marquess of Anglesey's Column, which rises above the Menai Strait with splendid views over the Anglesey estate. The people of Anglesey built this monument to the 1st Marquess in 1817 'in grateful commemoration of the distinguished military achievements of their countryman'. The footpath winds through a small wood to the column keeper's cottage, which has surely been borrowed from Hansel and Gretel. The tiny single-storey home of slate and stone is bedecked with flowers. There's no one at home, just a note pinned to the gate to request that the admission fee be popped through the letterbox in the front door.

At the foot of the column a door opens onto a staircase; it's a wooden spiral, something like you'd find in a medieval tower. A sign warns that a metal cable running down the stair's length at hand height is not a banister but a lightning conductor. A number of the ageing treads have wooden wedges banged into their joints and some of the planks have been replaced altogether by metal plates, none of which inspires confidence as you begin the 90-foot climb in circles into growing darkness. For a moment the daylight disappears almost completely, save for a shaft of the weakest sunshine a long way above. Towards the top of the tower, heading towards the growing light, the walls narrow and squeeze my shoulders. This is not a place to be stuck behind those of a nervous disposition or the generously upholstered.

After all the spiralling, the platform at the top feels unsteady at first. But it's been worth the effort. Below

me, in every direction, is one of the greatest views to be had in Britain, an unfolding landscape of fields and forests. From here I can see the meandering of the Menai Strait, both of its fine bridges leaping over the water. In the far distance lies the majesty of Snowdonia, the gathering wind not yet strong enough to blow away its stubborn cloud. Behind me, stretched out to the horizon, are the flat fields of Anglesey, the roads and railway racing in straight lines to the harbour at Holyhead. Far below, the ponies are now wide awake and, half-possessed by the wind, are running after each other playing a mad game of chase.

At the top of the column, a chance to make some notes and take in the stunning view.

 Beaumaris

True to his word and bang on time Dave the taxi driver is parked and waiting for his return fare when I get back down to the car park at Plas Newydd. The radio is on and the weather forecast about to begin. Dave hopes for rain because his customers are less likely to walk to the shops, but I want a clear day to walk up Snowdon. We're both disappointed, however: I won't be going up the mountain tomorrow or even the next day as the visibility is poor – the end of the week offers my best chance for a good view – and Dave won't get his rain.

We're now heading for the town described by George Borrow as 'second to none', just a short drive along the coast. The grand square stone houses of Beaumaris draw the tourists like bees to

111

nectar; when we get there we find them sauntering in the middle of the road. The car park is packed and the pavements are full. Dave slows down and smiles at the growing possibility of another fare when he drops me off outside the church.

St Mary's and St Nicholas's sits in the middle of the town, and its porch is home to a memorial to Siwan, also known as Princess Joan, wife of Llywelyn the Great and illegitimate daughter of King John. Their pairing was one of many attempts to bring the warring Welsh into the English establishment. She died in 1237 and was initially buried at Llanfaes Priory; her coffin was brought here at the Dissolution of the Monasteries.

Before they built the bridges across the water, travellers bound for London crossed the Menai Strait at low tide at Lavan Sands. Travellers journeying in the other direction, coming from the mainland, must have taken one look at the buildings in Beaumaris and assumed they'd crossed from Wales into England. This is one of those Welsh towns like Tenby in Pembrokeshire that are an intrinsic part of the Welsh landscape and yet, to me, not typically Welsh in architecture. Perhaps this should come as no surprise given the story of Beaumaris's foundation. Later, in Victorian times, the town pioneered experiments in social welfare. The jail in Beaumaris was the first in Britain with separate cells for men, women and children, and each cell had running water. Each prisoner was weighed on admission and given work and wages. As a gentle incentive to good behaviour for those on the other side of the wall, hangings in the jail could be viewed from the high street. It seemed to do the trick, since only two executions are recorded.

Beaumaris Castle

Two swans guard the entrance to Beaumaris Castle. They've made a nest in the moat nearby and seem rather cheesed off by the number of gawping bystanders – who, to be frank, are rather taking their lives into their hands by getting so close to the birds.

The castle grounds are full of dozens of children, some inquisitive and adventurous, bounding in and out of darkened arches, others screaming the place down, tired and querulous. Despite a generation's addiction to electronic entertainment and theme parks, the age-old pull of leaping around ancient ruins doesn't seem to have lost its thrill. Within these roofless walls a thousand childhood fantasies will be played out, hiding in dungeons and defending the battlements. Shell-shocked parents and grandparents sit on benches, counting the days to the new term.

The late afternoon is kind; it is one of those typically August days in Wales, first warm, then windy, then overcast with the promise of rain that never emerges. It will have been a good day for visitors and the town alike – it's too much of a gamble to risk the whole day on the beach so they've come here to explore. In such compromises Welsh holidays are made. After the re-enactments of horrible histories a few toddlers spend a good hour on the lawn within the castle walls trying to terrify tame young seagulls. The toddlers are too slow to catch the birds, and the birds are still too young to get much lift off. Who needs toys? 'See if you can catch a seagull, darling.'

The serious tourists come to the castle and to Caernarfon and Conwy with guidebooks and purposeful gait, stalking the gatehouse, chapel and outer ward, their imaginings of life past made easier by the multicoloured army of visitors patrolling the battlements. Wales isn't short of castles; a country surrounded by sea, bordering England and populated by professional troublemakers is always going to have its fair share. Beaumaris, however, is special, not just because of its pretty

KEEPING THE NATIVES AT BAY

*B*egun in 1295, Beaumaris was the last and largest royal stronghold to be built by Edward I in Wales, and completed the string of fortifications designed to rein in the Welsh begun in 1277. It marks an important moment in Welsh history and not just for Anglesey. Following the death of Llywelyn, Prince of Wales, in 1282, and the execution of his brother Dafydd the following year, Welsh resistance and the rule of the Welsh princes effectively came to an end. Edward laid down the statute of Rhuddlan, the pattern of a new, English-type administration based on shires and counties, sweeping away the historic Welsh system of cantrefi and commotes. This was not the last time local government reorganization would antagonize the Welsh.

So why build a castle here? This site was equidistant by water from the other fortifications at Caernarfon and Conwy and the old overland route from Chester to Holyhead. It was the crossing point to which travellers on their way to Ireland were ferried across the Menai Strait. No other place on Anglesey was better suited to becoming the centre of its English administration and business.

The native Welsh living in the small adjoining village of Llanfaes were cleared out and moved well away to a new territory called Newborough where they couldn't impede the rise of Beaumaris.

Whereas the construction of Caernarfon and Conwy was constrained by geology and geography, this flat marsh was unhindered by cliffs and rocks. A workforce numbering thousands of men began the construction of this squat castle in a concentric design of walls within walls. Its formidable defences included a wide, water-filled moat so the garrison could be provisioned from the sea. When construction work ceased in 1330, in part due to the Crown's commitments to Scotland, the upper floors and turrets of the inner tower remained unfinished.

Though Beaumaris was sufficiently usable to be garrisoned and besieged during the revolt of Owain Glyndwr in around 1400–1410, by 1539 the castle was reported to be 'much ruynous and ferre in decay'. In 1642, during the Civil War, Viscount Buckley shelled out the enormous sum of 3,000 pounds to repair the ruin for the Royalist cause, only to back the losing side.

Ducks and swans swim in the moat of Beaumaris Castle – the castle itself was never finished.

location but because the castle, with its near-perfect symmetry, is a World Heritage Site along with the Pyramids and the Taj Mahal.

Those without guidebooks wander around on a mystery tour, peering into roofless apartments and windowless chambers and climbing stone stairs that lead to nowhere. Fireplaces and doorways halfway up walls show more clearly than any guide could that where saplings now colour the grey stone, tapestries once warmed the walls. Although built to put the fear of God into the restless Welsh, even the impenetrable walls now exude a benign presence; it is a playground, a pleasure garden to be clambered over.

Beyond the castle gates, the main street is busy with shoppers and pushchairs. The empty high street premises found in so many Welsh towns are conspicuously absent here. It's a bit like walking back into the 1950s – the butcher and fishmonger are both advertising fishing bait (much to the delight of small boys, their rods and tackle box firmly clasped for an evening on the pier) and the clock shop man repairs my unthreading leather watchstrap.

Ye Olde Bull's Head Inn, where I stopped for a very civilized pint.

The lady in the kiosk at the end of the pier selling boat trips tries to persuade me to go on her next voyage, but we both look at the encroaching mist and know the last cruise of the day will be damp. She

says Anglesey council is about to close the leisure centre and that it's the only place to go in Beaumaris on a wet day. 'This is a damp and windy country all year round but they run it like the sun's always shining. It's all about budget cuts,' she says.

On the pebble shore, two dogs are fighting until a loud Mancunian shout makes everyone look round – including his hound, who races back to his side. The pier is lined with a hundred waterproofed tourists, some leaning over the railings watching the retreating tide beneath, others mesmerized by the well-practised seagulls swooping for every chip thrown in the air. There are no yachts now in the Menai Strait; sailors know when to head for home. The mainland across the water has disappeared beneath low cloud, and Anglesey is cut off and floating in the Irish Sea.

Turner visited Beaumaris in 1798 but he didn't produce his painting of the town until years later in 1835. His only known work of Anglesey must have been from half-remembered daydreams and hazy recollection. Even then he changed the landscape before him and produced a work that accurately depicted the castle but that greatly exaggerated the mountain backdrop. The shoreline too was brought forward for the sake of the composition – a cheaper method of refashioning the North Wales coast than that used by the Anglesey family's architects, builders and gardeners, I suppose.

I wander past the grand front doors of the pretty, three-storey pastel-coloured houses built by Joseph Hanson (the designer of the London cab), and turn up a passage leading to the main street and Ye Olde Bull's Head Inn. Built in 1472, this was the original posting house of the borough, commandeered by General Mytton who besieged the castle in 1645. Its low-lit, black-beamed, cream-walled little rooms don't look much changed since Dr Johnson and Charles Dickens checked in. A lone walker in safari shorts sits in the corner reading the paper over a pint. He looks relieved to have reached his destination: one foot, unbooted, is resting on a chair. Tomorrow there'll be blisters beneath those thick sweating socks.

The lid of the upright piano in the far corner is locked – though it doesn't have a sign like that at Plas Newydd, requesting punters not to play. Some time not so long ago a seriously bad piano player touring Anglesey must have left the population traumatized.

In one corner, around the small round table, two small children with their parents share a packet of crisps, and near them a middle-aged couple are deep in conversation about some family crisis. The landlord says he's having a successful summer in the pub and his room bookings are healthy too. He thinks the exchange rate and the recession have both kept tourists at home. Like Dave the taxi driver, he doesn't want the weather to be too hot because his customers will desert his bar for the beach. I tell him I'm planning to walk up Snowdon sometime this week when the weather forecast gives good visibility. He tells me of the news reports of French President Nicholas Sarkozy collapsing while out jogging today. 'A man can have too much exercise in later life,' he says, and then pours me a pint.

CHAPTER
SIX

From Anglesey to Llandudno

MENAI STRAIT ◉ PENRHYN ◉ CONWY ◉

LLANDUDNO ◉ THE GREAT ORME ◉

BODYSGALLEN HALL

T HE FORECASTERS on *Breakfast News* this morning promise 'fair' weather all week, starting dry and then becoming progressively sunnier every day. In Wales 'fair' seems to cover almost anything from drizzle to splendid sunshine – always pack a waterproof, then you can only be pleasantly surprised. If the forecasters are right, I should postpone my walk up Snowdon for another day or so and wait for perfect visibility. Since a day or two at leisure in North Wales beckons, I'm going to do what countless generations of holidaymakers have done and head for the seaside resort of Llandudno. It's not somewhere I know well. When we were kids growing up in Pembrokeshire, four hours' drive south, this was too far away to be on our list of days out. But for those who live in the north of England, in Manchester or Liverpool, and who fancy the thrill of going to another country, Llandudno is their personal playground.

OPPOSITE: *Seaside Special – Llandudno's traditional entertainment never goes out of fashion.*

The bus to Bangor railway station hustles along the side of the Menai Strait, where already there are a few yachts in full sail on the water, taking advantage of the early breeze. I've sailed up here in an old boat and it's not for the fainthearted: the water level of the Strait is constantly rising and falling, it's full of treacherous rocks trying to tear holes in your hull below the waterline and the currents are vicious. Easier just to avoid the water completely and get the bus over the bridge.

Out of the window St Tysilio's Church lies in the shadow of the bridge. This church is a monument to and reminder of the perils of crossing this Strait; it was here where travellers either prayed for a safe crossing or else gave thanks for getting to the other side intact.

We turn onto Menai Bridge. There can't be more than six inches leeway for the bus to squeeze past the huge pillars on either side. We slow down to a crawl for a piece of masterly driving that must have been done a thousand times and yet never gets any easier. But what we lose in speed we gain in scenery as we hover above the Menai Strait with one of the region's most glorious sights beneath us. Looking down I can see the water running in opposite directions and pooling in whirls. I'm the only tourist on board and positively salivating at my great good fortune at

117

BRIDGES TO ANGLESEY

*H*ung from wrought-iron chains (since replaced by stainless-steel cables) and dangling 100 feet above the water, this was the first suspension bridge in the world constructed to take heavy traffic. When it opened in 1826 it was also the longest bridge on earth. Conceived in the golden age of shipping, Thomas Telford's design allowed tall-masted vessels to pass beneath comfortably at high tide. I can't remember when I last saw a motorway bridge and thought that it really enhanced the landscape or had made an effort to blend in with the countryside. We tend to assume today that most civil engineering projects will inevitably brutalize the landscape, but this was made when function and beauty were still bedfellows.

It is indicative of Anglesey's importance as the pre-eminent route to Ireland that the Strait has not one but two of the world's most significant crossings. The Britannia Bridge opened in 1850, 24 years after Telford's. Designed by Robert Stephenson (son of George), this was the first major tubular bridge in the world and carried the new railway running from Chester to Holyhead. Having withstood the worst that the Irish Sea could throw at it for 120 years, in 1970 it had to be closed for four years after two local boys set fire to it.

The Menai Bridge, before 1930.

seeing this panorama – everyone else is local and, having seen it all before, have their noses deep in newspapers on the way to work.

It's five pounds fifty for a single ticket to Llandudno. Bangor station has yet to be given the client-focused makeover treatment – it's gritty, uncomfortable and functional, though it does at least offer shelter from the light drizzle that's just started. The platform has a handful of students waiting (as you'd expect in a university town). I don't know if they're doing summer courses or re-sits, but two of them are loaded up with all the usual detritus of life in digs that will be tricky to manhandle if they're not met at their destination.

This morning's newspaper has a feature about the seventieth anniversary this year of the nation's art treasures being removed from war-torn London for safe storage in Wales. Many of the country's most valuable paintings were taken from their galleries, packaged up, sent across the country and hidden in caves, far away from the bombing. Strange to think that while Hitler was using his efficient railways to pilfer the paintings and sculptures of France and Italy, over here we were using our railways to hide our art.

The train from Bangor to Birmingham International (calling at Llandudno) is a two-carriage affair. Though it's unlikely to figure in any of the world's great railway journeys, it's modern and clean and there's even a refreshment trolley with a mind of its own.

We hug the coast for most of the journey; the line runs along the narrow shelf of land beneath the cliffs and above the shore all the way to Llandudno. We're going past Penrhyn Castle now, partially hidden in the trees; it was built on the profits of West Indian sugar and Welsh slate hacked from these mountains and shipped all over the world. The house itself is an enormous Victorian pile built in the 1820s to look like an ancient Norman stronghold. Its medieval-looking arrow slits and murder holes conceal the technological advances installed in the house far ahead of their time; Penrhyn Castle boasted lavatories, hot and cold running water in the bathrooms, gas and oil lighting and even hot air ducts. Before Queen Victoria came to stay, a one-ton four-poster bed was commissioned, made from – what else? – slate. She refused to sleep on it. There's gratitude for you.

In the hills above us near Aber Falls stands the motte and bailey stronghold built by Llywelyn the Great, where he received Edward I's request to acknowledge his sovereignty over Wales. From the summit of Foel Fras on a clear day (and when the tide is low) you can clearly see the drying sands of Dutchman Bank that normally lurk treacherously below the surface of the water. Welsh legend has it that these coastal sands were once the fields, homes and farms of forgotten drowned towns.

We slow down before stopping abruptly in Llanfairfechan. One passenger gets off and no one joins us. Over the station wall, a groundsman is pacing behind his marking wheel like a ploughman, laying down the white lines of a football pitch before the start of the new season. It'll be a shame to mess up his perfectly striped green carpet. Looking out the other side, the shoreline is deserted apart from a woman throwing a ball into the surf for her sheep dog. Puffin Island, just off the tip of Anglesey, is coming into view; it won't see many boat trippers this morning – it's a breezy and damp affair in Conwy Bay.

THE SLATE INDUSTRY

While South Wales was making its fortune from coalfields, North Wales was making its own from slate. It's interesting to conjecture what course the Industrial Revolution would have taken without the immense contribution of both South and North Wales, since both of these materials formed the cornerstones of the Great British Century. In the age of Empire, buildings across the globe were roofed in Welsh slate, schoolchildren chalked on it (Baron Penrhyn had the contract), and memorial stones, steps, lintels and windowsills everywhere were fashioned from it.

There were darker sides to this global domination, of course – the Baron, also MP for Liverpool, was a staunch defender of the slave trade, and many of the workers closer to home were treated as little more than feudal serfs. By the late nineteenth century this had led to considerable ill feeling, and between 1900 and 1903 Penrhyn was the site of Britain's longest lockout. Although the slate industry never really recovered after the two World Wars, the Penrhyn quarry, the biggest in the world, is still being worked today.

The battlements of Conwy Castle, with Conwy Bay beyond.

Orange-clad track staff are working on the railway line at Penmaenmawr station, so we slow down to walking speed and clack noisily over some bumpy joins. The cars on the dual carriageway that we were overtaking a few moments ago now blur past our stationary carriage window. The disappearance of the engine din cues conversation from the table in front of me, where a middle manager is holding court with two underlings – who look decidedly bored with her corporate speak. The train slides slowly into movement again, but only just.

We pass through Dwygyfylchi slowly, past the backs of houses, shops and businesses. Travelling by train you always get to see all the things that people hide from the front of the house and end up in long grass at the back. Conwy Bay, apparently sitting in its own microclimate, is bathed in sunshine and its blue skies promise a better afternoon to come. We edge past the castle walls where a couple lying on the grass near the line seem surprised to see a train. The carriages cut incredibly close to the castle. Our reverence for the ancient is a modern notion – certainly here in Conwy the single-minded determination of the Victorian railway engineers to get from A to B as quickly as possible overrode any sentiment for the castle. As a result, one of the finest pieces of military architecture in Europe has been defiled three times by bridge builders.

A few minutes later and we've arrived at Llandudno Junction. Here we must change trains for the remainder of the journey to Llandudno. I press what I think is the exit button to unlock the carriage door, only to open the toilet. Finding the correct button, I hastily disembark, hoping no one was watching. There's a 20-minute wait for the next train.

A gaggle of teenage girls sit on one of the platform benches plotting their day's campaign: some shopping, a little lunch and then – a giggle – perhaps some boys. They slip effortlessly between languages, though the more indiscreet confessions are in low murmured Welsh. They text endlessly while talking and use the screens in their mobiles to touch up their make-up. A seagull lands on the middle of the oil-slicked track in front of us to peck at something unmentionable and the passengers stop their conversations to see whether it'll get squashed by the oncoming train.

Fortunately for the seagull the Llandudno service shows up six minutes late. In truth it would have been quicker to walk or get a taxi but, like a good tight-fisted West Walian, I've paid for my ticket and I'm going to get my money's worth. The three-carriage train disgorges half a dozen passengers before a similar number of us board.

Past Deganwy now and its new marina – a hoarding advertises that the waterside show home is now open for viewing. The lucky inhabitants of these townhouses can walk out of their sitting rooms onto their jetties and into their boats. The golfers are out in force in their Rupert Bear trousers, and behind them shiny white plastic cruisers bob at their moorings.

The seats and tables of the train are littered with paper cups and plastic sandwich wrappers, which within moments of our departure are scooped up by a conscientious attendant who throws them all into a black sack. This line has the cleanliness and efficiency you'd expect of an airline rather than a railway. 'The trains would be so much cleaner if it wasn't for the passengers,' the attendant complains. An automated voice announces that Llandudno is the next stop, and no sooner have I stowed my rucksack and got comfortable than it's time to get off again.

Llandudno

It was by railway that the vast majority of Llandudno's visitors would have got here until the 1960s. Their holidays of perhaps a week or two from the factories of Victorian England would have begun with the anticipation and excitement of a short railway journey from the industrial cities to the coast, each family carrying a couple of small suitcases. I wanted to hang out of the train window as we used to do when we were kids, but air-conditioned carriages (and health and safety regulations too, no doubt) mean the doors no longer have sliding windows. Arriving, the holidaymakers of the past would have taken a brisk walk along Vaughan Street, the children running far ahead, unable to contain their excitement to see the sea at the end of the road.

This is one of Britain's great seaside resorts, the kind of place where everyone used to take holidays before the Costas muscled in. Despite the rise of the foreign holiday, a couple of weeks in Llandudno never went away for the thousands of tourists who continue to come here as they've always done – it's just that you never read about people who holiday in places like this in the celebrity magazines. *Seaside Special* may have disappeared from our television screens but the party continued in resorts like Llandudno. Just beyond the railway station car park on the generous wide roads, coaches from the north of England roll up outside dozens of hotels, dropping off another 50 people and taking another load home. There's no flight to the sun involved, no certainty of a tan, yet it is honest in what it offers: a cheap break by the sea for hard-working people desperate for a few days away. Many have been coming since they were children trotting

OVERLEAF: *The seafront at Llandudno, as viewed from the Great Orme.*

along the Prom with their parents in factory fortnight. Now they come with their own families, maybe even stay in the same hotels and walk the same walks, to be reassured of the past even if the future looks less certain.

Until 1854 Llandudno was no more than a village. Then the local landowners, the Mostyn family, began building on the marsh and sand, creating the purpose-built seaside resort that stands today. The Mostyns and their associates developed Llandudno to make money, to take advantage of the increasingly wealthy workers of industrial England. But the project was also informed by a genuine sense of interest in the welfare of its visitors. The town is laid out on a grid plan, rather like Pembroke Dock where I grew up – except here it follows the curve of the seashore. Just as the Butes of Cardiff insisted that their architect should bring a unity to the design of the city and its surroundings, the Mostyns too exerted a strong influence over the aesthetics of their development. Mostyn Street's three- and four-storey buildings are generous and tasteful structures, and the cast-iron verandas and lamps added greatly to the sumptuousness of their new town.

The season here begins in earnest at Easter. Although it may be too cold to sit out for long at this time of year, the occasional day will be kind enough for a good walk on the Prom. It'll be conference-goers and the retired who come here in the weeks after the school holidays – the conference business in particular is crucial to the fickle world of tourism. The retirees wait for the quiet of term time and the lower tariffs. July and August bring the crowds, when the pavements are full and the average age drops by at least a decade. By September the pensioners are back, chancing a late summer holiday before the 'Turkey and Tinsel' breaks start in the months leading up to Christmas.

A bench on the Prom (if you can find an empty one) is the best place to watch Britain on holiday. We have been rewarded with a bright sunny afternoon with a stiff breeze – just right for flying kites on the shore, though too cool to lie and sunbathe without a windbreak. The distant clouds over Snowdon will have caught everyone's eye and made this afternoon rather than tomorrow the day of the beach outing. Every moment of brightness is savoured in case the rain heads this way.

We are not a glamorous set, we Brits; we don't dress up to go to the beach or for a walk on the Prom. Eschewing the high fashion of Cannes or Monte Carlo, we quite reasonably figure that getting sand or ice cream on your best clothes would be a shame, so we don't bother. Instead it's sensible shoes, a cardy and a mac. If there is a fashion to be picked out from the crowds it is the football shirt, most likely in the colours of Manchester United.

A dozen or so elderly couples, arm in arm as much for support as out of affection, have passed me, silently patrolling well-trodden routes. They have no need for conversation; having said all there is to say, they know what each other is thinking without the need for words. Some sitting on the benches are here on their own, staring in to the middle distance and remembering.

There are legions of young families here too. Couples navigate pushchairs heavy with sleeping tots, having discovered the age-old prescription to stop childhood screaming: a bolt of fresh sea air and a soothing trundle along the Prom. Not for them the endurance test of the airport, three hours' check-in and a flight with your legs folded behind your head. Not when the kids are so young, but perhaps next year if things at work start to look up. Llandudno is full of the very young and the very old, but I haven't seen many teenagers. It isn't cool to go on holiday with your mum and dad once you get to a certain age. But they'll come back here one day, to remember holidays when they were little, or perhaps when they can't face the airport with small children experience. Then they'll come back and complete the circle.

Llandudno's old-fashioned musicals and variety shows always pull in the crowds.

This is unvarnished Britain, the Britain of most people. Not terribly glamorous, not always beautiful, but honest. These aren't the people reported in the newspapers, the magazines or on the television but the un-Photoshopped, unremarkable, ordinary and hard-working Britons who are determined to enjoy a well-deserved holiday by the sea.

The kiosks are full of buckets, spades and butterfly nets – or are they fishing nets? All the vital equipment required for a holiday by the sea is here. The pier is in good condition too, which is quite an achievement given how many British resorts have lost their piers to dereliction or fire. Diane Delaney has a kiosk halfway down the pier; her wind chimes hanging outside the door sing in the breeze. Most of the stock is outside the kiosk; the inside is too small for much more than a counter and the till. She says visitor numbers are good this year but people look rather than buy. 'July was hopeless and wet,' she says. 'They just don't come out when it's raining.' She's hoping that August will be more lucrative.

The end of the pier wouldn't be complete without a show, and in Llandudno it's a singer who performs endlessly without applause to the seated crowd eating their chips. The end of the pier proper, though, belongs to the anglers, who have paid a fee for a permit to spend the day fenced

Left: *Llandudno Pier in about 1910.*

Opposite: *The tram footplate on the way up the Great Orme.*

off from the public. Two dozen of them, almost shoulder to shoulder and mindful of the human flesh all around them, cast their lines with the discipline of ballet dancers so as not to hook their compatriots. The music must be scaring the fish, however, because no one seems to have caught anything – even the expectant seagulls have decamped to gobble up a feast near the chip eaters. A couple of paper bags, napkins and plastic trays breeze past them before burial at sea.

 The Great Orme

Overlooking the beach at Llandudno is an enormous limestone headland known as the Great Orme. The views from the top are remarkable, and all visitors to Llandudno should try to get up there. If you don't fancy the rather gruelling walk, however, the tram is the cheat's route. I've just got to the terminus, which is quiet – just a Jewish family battling with a folding pushchair and three elderly Italian men who are attempting to out-shout each other. All aboard, and it's immediately obvious that the wooden slatted benches were designed for a shorter-legged generation; knees touch knees from the opposite seat, and the bench isn't quite generous enough for twenty-first-century backsides.

A metallic alarm sounds and the driver standing in the centre of the open footplate swings a heavy wheel the size of a dinner plate. Slowly we grind into the daylight to the sound of metal on metal and creaking woodwork straining at its stays. The tram makes quiet progress ignoring the white road markings of the street. The hill we are starting to climb is steep enough to induce heart failure and reason enough to build a tram. The traffic discovers an uncustomary politeness, and just as steam gives way to sail on the sea, the cars give priority to our clanging progress. Up Belle Vue Terrace now towards Halfway station where we'll change to another tram to take us up the single track to the summit. To the sea side of us on the cliff the cable cars whizz past like gnats on wires.

As we move beyond the line of houses, gorse and heather begin to line the route. Looking up, I can see dog walkers and kite fliers on the clifftop, along with the infamous goats brought here by Lord Mostyn a hundred years ago.

There's a short wait at Halfway for the next service – just time to walk through the tram exhibition to the summit platform. Here the giant's toys of Victorian engineering lie on the floors of the workshop and hang on the walls. These outsize wheels, spanners and axles look so antiquated in our microchip world and yet these relics will outlast most of today's technology. There certainly won't be many computers made today in daily use a hundred years from now.

I'm now on the next tram, and it doesn't take us long to reach the top of the Great Orme, 18 minutes after boarding at the bottom of the hill. The first thing I see as soon as I walk out of the terminus is distant Snowdon, miles and miles away and still shrouded in cloud – or perhaps it's a heat haze? Wherever you travel in North Wales the mountain follows you around like the eyes of a painting. It would have been a mistake to climb it today; I'll wait until tomorrow or maybe even the day after.

At the summit of the Great Orme, 679 feet above sea level, it's a clear day and a beautiful one at that. Taking in the view, it's like looking at a three-dimensional map of my journey so far. Out to the west I can see back to Anglesey and Puffin Island across Conwy Bay, and behind me the long wide sweep of the North Wales coast hides Colwyn Bay, Rhyl and Prestatyn. There's a model boating pool on West Shore, at this height looking more like a grey pocket handkerchief pulled flat and left above the shingle. It's a sign of more innocent times when holiday entertainment didn't need to be electrical or expensive; it was dug on the site of an earlier pool built in about 1850 and used then for washing iron ore.

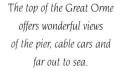

The top of the Great Orme offers wonderful views of the pier, cable cars and far out to sea.

In this old country you don't have to wander far to find archaeological treasures but on the Great Orme you don't have to wander anywhere at all: in this tiny patch of land you can find evidence of practically every age of man's story on earth. This was home to prehistoric man, the Romans came here to mine the copper, and St Tudno (from whom the town takes its name) founded his monastic cell here. There's a Neolithic burial chamber, an Iron Age fort, a medieval settlement and a Bronze Age copper mine – all within a mile of the headland. Modern Llandudno may have been a Victorian development, but the Victorians were just the latest in a long line to recognize that this spectacular mountain of rock sticking out in the sea was something special.

There is a queue for the cable car, a British queue, patiently waiting in order. No queue jumping or loud complaining, just a few grumbles under the breath to satisfy any pent-up annoyance. Some of the crowd wear raincoats – two elderly ladies have matching ones – and a couple of dads are wearing the same T-shirts and shorts.

The trip by cable car covers about a mile, taking us all the way down the headland to the side of Llandudno Pier. Nearing the top of the outdoor queue, the snake of passengers disappears into a tight squeeze past the ticket office and then the turnstile of the terminal building. Children clambering aboard with their parents squeak with delight as the car clunks precariously before tipping forward and then escapes from the din of the wheel house behind.

I'm now seated in my car, which is completely open to the elements. In an age muffled by 'health and safety' it feels pleasantly adventurous as the 40-year-old mechanicals fly you by wire at walking speed high above the headland. Far out on the horizon a seascape unchanged for an eternity is now home to a windfarm – though today they look fairly static, unmoved by the breeze that is rocking the cable cars. I look down to see 20-odd horned goats chewing the grass 60 feet beneath us. They are standing their ground in the face of some barking dogs who are clearly unnerved that they don't frighten them. These goats were a present from the Shah of Iran to Queen Victoria. She did what any self-respecting monarch would do when presented with a dodgy present that would clearly make life hell – she offloaded them onto someone else, in this case the Welsh, in the shape of Lord Mostyn. There is no noise up here except for when we pass through a support pylon which causes the rollers on the cable car's gantry to shudder violently.

After a few minutes the wide sweep of Llandudno's pastel hotels that demarcates the seafront comes slowly into view. In front of them the welcoming red carpet of tarmac that runs the length of the prom and, reaching out to the sea, the pier. With its silver roofs and black legs, it reminds me of a bonneted old lady lifting her skirts for a paddle.

From up here I can see clearly that most of the shore is shingle; it's only the stretch nearest the pier that is loaded with sand. Every patch of ground above the tide line is specked with people, some sitting on deckchairs, others lying on rugs or behind windbreaks – you can hear the burble of play from here. A wooden jetty that from this distance looks no wider than a plank holds passengers waiting for two boats offering pleasure cruises around the bay.

We arrive at the cable-car terminus on Happy Valley Road. At the nearby Grand Hotel you can (for a supplement) upgrade your booking to include access to a 'superior dining room' with sea view and better food. The billboard opposite has posters pinned up of the forthcoming week's entertainment. This is the cruel barometer of light entertainment: you won't have heard of most of the acts (maybe they're on their way up), while some of the headliners you may have assumed had already gone to the Great Green Room in the sky.

Prince Edward Square is a cacophony of competing voices, each pleading for your custom. The Punch and Judy man mesmerizes a small generation sitting respectfully beneath his short wooden tower, each of them more used to entertainment from an electronic box. Meanwhile the boatman announces at the top of his voice that this next ride will be the last one of the day (though once the vessel is full he sells more tickets for the next one departing in half an hour). As his boat leaves shore he motors past a dingy making slow progress across the water, the dying wind no longer quite enough to fill her blue sails.

A vintage AEC single-decker bus, complete with two-tone green coachwork and complaining double declutching gears, waits to take its next load of passengers on a magical mystery tour. In the 1930s tourists would walk past billboards offering charabanc trips to see FIVE MOUNTAINS and FIVE LAKES and also for AFTERNOON TEA WITH THE LORD OF THE MANOR. The manor in question is Bodysgallen Hall; the lord used to open up for the tourists to make a few

THE TWO FACES OF LLANDUDNO

Llandudno has two beaches: the North Shore, which has the fine Victorian buildings perched on its edge, and behind it the West Shore, which rarely makes the postcards. From here it looks as though the West Shore is windier, the lines on the water give it away. This is the less familiar face of Llandudno, the one that seems to be preferred by kite fliers and joggers. West Shore was once an industrial area dedicated to sorting ore from the Great Orme's copper mines. It was in this industrial area that Dean Liddell purchased a plot of land from the Mostyn Estate to build his house Penmorfa, now long gone. The Mostyns decided to develop the North Shore first, and the West Shore never got the design treatment of its fine terraced houses and it lacks the ordered formality of its neighbour. The area's most famous visitor was Dean Liddell's daughter Alice, the inspiration behind **Alice in Wonderland**, who spent her summers here. In 1933 Lloyd George came here to unveil a statue to the White Rabbit – though the council have always been careful not to suggest that the author Lewis Carroll was a Llandudno visitor.

quid. Sadly he no longer lives there, and the bus trips no longer run. But I'm going to collect a hire car for the rest of my journey and drop in at Bodysgallen for dinner.

Bodysgallen Hall

Bodysgallen Hall has been in the headlines in Wales recently as the latest acquisition of the National Trust. This house was one of the homes of the Mostyn family who laid out modern-day Llandudno; like the family, it has been at the heart of the area's history for centuries.

The narrow lane meanders sideways up a steep hill to a stone house hidden by tall trees. Nobody builds houses on the tops of hills in Wales unless they want them to double up as lookout towers. As the trees clear I can see that the house, considerable in size, does indeed look like a defensive castle though the usual harsh lines, mean windows and bleak surroundings are absent here. The building is breathtakingly striking, a centuries-old riddle in stone; the fountains and formal garden beneath look magnificent. Bodysgallen's grounds include a rare seventeenth-century parterre of box hedges; even standing this far away you can smell its sweet-scented herbs. I can also see a rockery with a cascade, a walled rose garden and several follies.

Bodysgallen Hall is a wonderful mishmash of styles and periods, built over 600 years.

The house has had extension built upon extension over 600 years, but despite these additions it has kept its sturdy conservative style. The name may mean either 'house among the thistles' or 'the house of Cadwallon' (the sixth-century chieftain). The oldest part of the house is the five-storey tower, which looks as though it dates from the thirteenth century and may have been built as a watchtower for nearby Conwy Castle.

THE IMPACT OF THE FIRST WORLD WAR

The First World War saw landowners and lords of the manor turn into army recruitment officers. Colonel Henry Mostyn was no exception, and beginning with his own staff he raised the 17th battalion of the Royal Welsh Fusiliers. He used to parade his men in the park to the north of the house – the oak tree in the centre of the field marks where they used to gather. Under his command, the small army of land workers who kept the house and gardens running left behind their spades and shovels,

tied cottages and certainty, and followed him to the trenches.

Many never returned to the fields of Bodysgallen, and those who did survive realized the world extended far beyond this 200-acre estate. The end of the war in 1918 in a sense marked the end of the great house gardens and landed estates, along with the six-and-a-half-day working weeks and the near-serfdom that blighted the lives of many of those who worked in them.

The two main storeys of the early seventeenth-century block house a large entrance hall and an equally large room above, now the drawing room. Both rooms have two fireplaces, a main one and another in a bay in the corner. It is thought that the latter was for the use of the nanny and children so that the master, his wife and guests could enjoy the heat of the main blaze undisturbed.

The family archives include a 1823 receipt from John Williams of St Asaph for the pioneering installation of a water closet. By this time Bodysgallen had already become an architectural jumble, with brick chimneys and Georgian sliding windows. It was rescued and restored by the formidable Lady Augusta Mostyn at the turn of the century as a wedding present for her son, Henry (she was also the driving force behind the development of Llandudno). Many Victorian restorations border on the criminal, but Lady Augusta's work was remarkable in its sensitivity for the vernacular architecture of the house.

Things were changing, however, and the radical social changes of the twentieth century, brought about largely by two World Wars, upset the status quo. The first death knell for this house came with the passing of Lady Augusta in 1912. Then, following the death of Colonel Henry in 1938 and his widow in 1949, their eccentric son Ieuan Mostyn succeeded and the decline accelerated. His niece sold the property in 1969, at which point it became a private guesthouse in growing need of considerable funds to rescue the failing fabric and gardens.

Just past the thick entrance door the green striped library is slightly faded. It feels as though the master will return from hunting soon. Ancient houses have a unique scent, a mixture of candlewax on wood, centuries of burnt logs and the smell of leather holding together the damp pages of books. Despite the fact that it is now a hotel, it still feels like a well-loved private home. Matthew Johnson, the director, pops his head around the door and offers to take me on a quick tour. He suggests that the house had its origins in 1250 as a watchtower and that since it has been the seat of several of the big families of North Wales: the Wynns, the Vaughans and the Mostyns. The motto of the last of these, inscribed above the fireplace reads: 'In God we have everything'. On a first glance around the panelled walls and mullioned windows, they were probably right.

When the estate was sold in 1969, some of the land was broken into small parcels and the contents auctioned off. Historic Houses bought the property itself in 1979, by which time the parterre garden was a wasteland and the tack room had a tree growing through the roof. A long restoration ensued that would take 30 years of scouring auctions for long-lost paintings and fittings – when the Mostyn family's other seat went under the hammer at Sotheby's, Bodysgallen regained some of its original chattels. Inevitably, the house is a gathering of disparate furniture and paintings not all necessarily original to it. But it all seems to come together to create a pleasing and complete home.

The Gardens at Bodysgallen

Outside in the splendid grounds, Robert Owen, the head gardener, is busy dead-heading roses on the terrace closest to the house. He kindly offers to shows me around some of the parkland and garden that keep him busy. He came for an interview on a Saturday morning 28 years ago and never left. He has watched the restoration of the gardens from waist-high jungle to their present manicured Eden. There were once 14 full-time gardeners here; now they manage with three.

'The garden isn't as it was a hundred years ago,' Robert explains. 'Plant technology has moved on since Victorian times and the varieties we plant now are better suited to the soil and climate: they are more hardy, frost resistant and better performing.' His two colleagues are below us, beginning the three-day campaign that is cutting all the grass.

Robert is something of a celebrity, a guest speaker at the country's top gardening clubs, but he's wistful about the changing role of this garden's staff over the century. The gardener's ascendancy in Britain has been achieved through huge effort. At one time they were seen as no more than an extension of the household's equipment.

The formal garden is the size of two rugby pitches placed side by side. The breeze that would normally swipe the blooms off delicate plants is stalled by the ten-foot-high stone wall that runs around the edge of the garden. The lengths to which the wealthy would go to change the weather and create their own climate are extraordinary. The enormous size of the formal garden is broken up by low hedges to create four quarters of roughly symmetrical shape. Each quarter has at its centre a climbing rose supported by a wooden obelisk, flanked by four borders containing a dozen rose bushes. The paths that run around and across the formal garden are punctuated by small trees and standard roses; the shrubs all bloom white. All of this is set off against mature forestry on the perimeter of the estate with a cutting through the growth to show Snowdonia's mountains in the far distance.

In the middle of the wall at the end of the formal garden a green door beckons as it might have done to Alice, had she come here on her summer visits to Llandudno. Passing under its low arch a wonderland of fruit and vegetables beckons. This is the produce garden, the engine of a great house beyond the pretty flower façade. Again the garden is quartered, but compared to its neighbour's restraint of colours this is a riot of rainbows. Dahlias in purple, yellow, pink and gold are staked with bamboo to save their fat heads from falling off their pin legs; apples (still a month too early to pick off and bite into) are grown along wires. On the other side of the garden, through another low doorway, two fat rabbits sit by the compost and cuttings heap, waiting to see if we forget to shut the door. In neat rows, marrows, turnips and carrots line up behind swedes, shallots and onions – all kept in order behind the chicken wire fence that marks the battleline between gardener and rabbit. On the opposite side to the vegetables, a wire mesh fruit cage is home to redcurrants and raspberries, which shoot up their frame untroubled by birds. The only intrusion into paradise is the distant rumble of traffic on the A55.

I tell Robert that I want to climb Snowdon tomorrow or the next day but want perfect visibility. He tells me to leave it for a few more days, like his grass.

Dinner is as you'd expect: a civilized affair in an oak-panelled dining room with damask tablecloths, looking out through mullioned windows towards Snowdonia under a pink sky. The meal's crowning glory is a cheese course featuring one that smells like an un-hosed farmyard but tastes like heaven. My fellow guests are a mixture of foreign families and Britons on holiday. In the bar after dinner the night manager Mike Jordan offers to show me the 'unseen Hall' that is usually off limits to visitors. The Hall's rooms, corridors and floors are inevitably an uneven, irregular warren, the product of organic growth over centuries, but Mike's keys take us to an even narrower uncarpeted behind-the-scenes hall of winding staircases and endless walls without paintings or tapestries. These are not passages built for guests but for service. After what seems like a five-storey climb up the narrowest of spiral staircases we come to another low door. This time it opens outwards into the blackest of darkness, making the stairs look well lit.

We are standing unsteadily on a flat roof outdoors in what is at first complete darkness. Then our eyes gradually adjust to the light and begin to pick out shapes, then colours. We are standing on the top of the ancient watchtower, looking out across hills and valleys for miles in every direction. Straight ahead is low-lit Conwy Castle. Here, at the top of this tower, night watchmen would have kept a vigil, blowing on their cold hands, stamping their feet and keeping their eyes peeled for advancing trouble. Snowdon sits magisterially supreme and unconquerable, illuminated by the moon shining through cloud. How many nights must those watchmen have stood here scanning the hills and praying the land would remain at peace at least until daylight?

The gardens at Bodysgallen are some of the finest in North Wales. Parts of them date back to the seventeenth century.

133

B-Roads to Portmeirion

EGLWYSBACH ◉ GWYDIR CASTLE ◉ BETWS-Y-COED ◉

T MAWR WYBRNANT ◉ DOLWYDDELAN CASTLE ◉

BLAENAU FFESTINIOG ◉ PLAS BRONDANW ◉

PORTMEIRION

*I*T'S NOT EASY travelling around Wales on B-roads any more. It's not that they've all been turned into motorways – after all, we still only have part of the M4 – but rather that the B-road network has been slowly fractured by other developments. Upgrades and improvements, bypasses and dual carriageways have all left behind a fragmented, discontinuous toddle of short wanders off the beaten track. A trip down a promising B-road will often turn out to be short-lived as your route turns into an A-road or even (heaven forbid) a dual carriageway. Given the brevity of these routes, like a good cigar or a fine wine they are to be savoured while driving on them – and that's not something that you can say of the weekday commute. That you can't easily cross from north to south or east to west on the B-roads in Wales makes finding these routes even more enjoyable.

OPPOSITE: An attractive fountain at Gwydir Castle.

◉

A good example of a really satisfying B-road is the B5106. A long, straight road, it was probably used by the Romans who built a spa at Trefriw – you need a good spa after a long march. It starts with great promise in Conwy near the castle, it wanders along the river valley following – as most B-roads do – the natural contours of the land, and then glides past Gwydir Castle at Llanrwst. But then the inevitable happens: it enters Betws-y-coed, but never comes out. To go anywhere else from here you need to take an A-road. So your B-road bagger is a connoisseur of brief pleasures.

In the tarmac comedy scale, your B-road is a middle-sized Ronnie Barker, while motorway, dual carriageway or A-road is a towering John Cleese. And both cock a snook at the Ronnie Corbett track-like inadequacy of an unclassified road.

Like the water running off the mountains, most Welsh roads take the easiest route to their destination – it's simpler than trying to hack your way through rock. The soft, flat land of Anglesey offers the road builder few challenges, but the jagged landscape of Snowdonia has always forced history's civil engineers to follow the geology, snake around the side of hills, and bend around the streams and rivers. As a result, B-roads encourage diversion and slow you down enough to be able to savour the scenery. They invite you to stop and look around. So it is that a little flag at the side of the road signposting Eglwysbach Agricultural Show catches my eye and piques my curiosity. Surely I can afford a diversion for an hour or so.

Eglwysbach Agricultural Show

For one day a year, come rain or shine, the four flat fields that lie beneath the hills in Eglwysbach exchange grazing animals and agricultural instruments for a tapestry of marquees, exhibition stands, show rings and two temporary car parks. You can see the show as you curl down the Hiraethlyn Valley, like a medieval tournament waiting for the jousting to begin. Show-goers will be relieved to see that the ground is hard and yellowing for want of rain – they have been spared the usual mud-caked waddle in Wellingtons and a day dodging the showers.

With greater accountability and efficiency than many police forces could muster, the members of Eglwysbach and District Agricultural and Horticultural Show Society have taken control of parking arrangements. Yellow- and orange-vested teachers and builders find themselves directing traffic, and do so with a ruthless logic. No waiting and no double-parking here – show traffic is waved into a field and given firm instructions.

The day begins early in the countryside and the first classes were on show before the crowds even arrived. Mr S. M. Richardson from East Yorkshire has already judged the Shire Horses (better to invite judges from far away than to risk any accusations of bias). The first prize was 30 pounds but what counts is not the cash bounty – which has remained unchanged through decades of inflation and Mr Wilson's devaluation – but the award itself. Mr Kevin Naughton from Crewe will judge the Jerseys, which right now are being chamois leathered; Mr Birch from Stafford will decide the best Simmental Cattle, and Mr Robert Shaw has travelled down from the Wirral to deliver his verdict on the Herefords.

The smooth running of the day is the culmination of months of meetings and committee gatherings. Competitions will run efficiently as they always have, and no one will be paid a penny for their labours. Of course it helps that there are 50 members of the committee (nothing much gets done in Wales without a committee – it is in the long tradition of the miners and the chapel that every voice should be heard, even if it is not always listened to).

In a line of stalls beneath the cooling shadow of the trees, the Welsh Black Cattle have been washed and shampooed until their fur is bouffant. The exhausted lady farmer in overalls and boots, bucket and sponge in hand, must have been up at first light – now that the beasts are ready she takes herself off to clean up before their joint appearance in the ring.

The cattle and sheep classes are diminished this year because of restrictions on livestock movement, but even then the classes are substantial. As you'd expect in this part of the world, the sheep pen takes up the biggest display. The rosettes awarded are stuck firmly onto the wooden pen for all to see. Any prize today will increase the price the farmer can ask for his stock – some may even sell their flocks. A 'Best in Show' will be a stay of execution for the lambs behind the fence – no prospect of a trip to the slaughterhouse for them; instead they have a life of breeding to look forward to. There'll be a party in the winning farmhouse tonight and a similar celebration out in the yard too, I shouldn't wonder – it's not every day you exchange a death sentence for a life of professional reproduction.

The marquees and tents at Eglwysbach Agricultural and Horticultural Show.

I'm now standing by the horse ring, watching the smart bowler-hatted judges. In their suits, ties and bowler hats they're probably the only men left in Britain who dress this way – especially now that the City of London has gone casual. They watch the junior riders canter in circles. In tweed jackets, ties and jodhpurs, the riders whisper pleadings to their mounts in the hope that best behaviour might win attention and even a rosette. You could have sat at this ringside on these bales of hay a hundred years ago and watched this same spectacle – nothing much has changed about this age-old ritual.

Who would want to have to judge between three children riding their ponies, though? Watched from the rope by their parents, hearts in mouths, they are each asked to walk on, stand and then gallop. A full ten minutes pass as the judge looks at animal and rider, before beckoning the winner forward and awarding the red rosette. Judging done, the competitors ride around the ring once more before heading back to the horsebox, triumphant or disheartened. A white-coated elderly lady with spade and bucket walks into the ring to shovel up the evidence of the last competition. The adult carriage drivers wait their turn patiently before entering the show ring for their moment of scrutiny.

A waft of hot dogs and onions fills the air before being dismissed by the hot oil from a complaining generator. Wandering past the NAME THE DOG, HOOK A DUCK and AUNTIE AUDREY'S FRUIT CAKE stalls, women slow and stop to chat and buy. The men, on the other hand, walk purposefully towards VINTAGE TRACTORS, where a century of machinery cherished in sheds enjoys a rare day out in the sun. Here polished red Fordsons and little grey Fergusons, cleaner than they ever were in their working lives, stand alongside other relics of farming past.

There won't be television coverage or much in the newspapers, but in Eglwysbach this is an important event, a highlight of the calendar. It's often said that community spirit is dying out but only by those who never go to places like Eglwysbach. The show is the spirit of the community and although in Wales fewer of us than ever work in the countryside, there is something inside all of us that has a need to turn off the main road and just for a day reconnect with our rural roots. A long way from the celebrity talent shows and the newspapers' latest tattle, here they're just getting on as they have always done with what really matters: celebrating ordinary life in the Welsh countryside.

Gwydir Castle

The shire horses and the Grand Parade will swell the crowds this afternoon, but the journey calls out so it's back on the B5106. They're still cutting the hay in the fields past Caerhun. They'll miss the show this morning – but business is business even on the farm. Through Dolgarrog now and finally, hiding in the trees guarding the western crossing of the Afon Conwy at Llanrwst, is Gwydir Castle.

The eighteenth-century zoologist, writer and traveller Thomas Pennant pondered the origins of the name Gwydir and suggested that it came from 'Gwaed-dir' or 'bloody land', referring to the succession of battles fought here. The area was already notable in the Dark Ages for skirmishes fought between rival princes: battles waged here in 610 and 954 had resulted in slaughter on a staggering scale. It had quietened down by the time the great writer John Leland came in 1536 and said: 'Gwydir lieth two bowshots above the river Conwy.'

There's no car park at the castle and no visitor centre, just a bell to ring after you've walked though the old door at the side of the castle. Judy Corbett comes to the entrance of the private wing of the building that she has rescued from ruin and welcomes you into a thousand years of Welsh history. There's no guided tour or audio description, just a small fee and a pointer to the public wings. You can wander around under your own steam and stay as long as you want.

This is not a castle of the Conwy kind, with huge battlements and impenetrable keeps, but rather a manorial home that is as modest as it is intriguing. The wisteria-clad, honey-stoned walls form two L-shaped wings that look out over a formal garden to the front. The medieval mix of chimneys, turrets, tower, great hall, courtroom and bedrooms are more country house than fortress. The peacocks prancing past the sundial keep an eye on your progress across the gravel. Their ancient screech serves as a sort of living burglar alarm.

The oak door to the public quarters looks like two old doors that have grown together; their bolted planks are fantastically heavy. Entering, I feel as though I'm intruding into someone's private quarters. There are no ropes barring my wanderings, I'm free to come and go wherever I want. Three logs are glowing red and white on the hearthstone in the enormous fireplace, which must be large enough to stand in. A chair, close enough to feel the heat from the flames in a cool room even on a hot day, is pushed to one side as though its sitter might return at any moment. A set of antlers over the fireplace points at the wooden staircase at the other end of the room. It's cooler and darker than the bright day outside and my eyes take a moment to adjust to life inside a medieval house. There is a smell too, the scent of history, of wax polish and old fabric. The small, mullioned windows make the interior dark. Gwydir's life has been lived in shadows and flickers of firelight. Sitting here by the fire it's easy to be transported back in time to see that even simple tasks like reading, writing and sewing must have all been carried out during the day sitting in the window or else squinting by fire

or candlelight.

There's been some form of manorial complex on this site since the fourteenth century. However, many historians point out that the oldest things at Gwydir are not the house, but two enormous yew trees near the terrace – they are probably between 600 and a thousand years old. The first resident here was possibly Hywel Coetmore, a captain of the Welsh longbowmen who fought under the Black Prince at the Battle of Poitiers in 1356. He was clearly a man of impeccable taste – not that you'd want to argue with an archer on such trivial matters.

The estate really grew, however, thanks to the efforts of the Wynn dynasty, founded by Meredith ap Ieuan ap Robert. Meredith lived in a Wales dominated by violence and bloodshed of civil war and internecine feuding. He lived his early life in the Conwy Valley – a notorious den of thieves and murderers, but one that he almost single-handedly brought under control. He was also a significant figure on the battlefields of France in the Battle of the Spurs and at the siege of Tournai in 1513. Back home he set his mind to building the new Gwydir on the site of the earlier manor house. He died in 1525 having fathered over 30 children with three

Gwydir Castle may not have battlements and a towering keep, but it has more than its fair share of mystery and intrigue.

wives and four concubines – a more agreeable end perhaps than his father's untimely death from plague at the age of 31.

Significant though the lives of the owners of Gwydir were, the most important figure in the house's history was a small boy who came here for lessons. Bishop William Morgan – as this child would one day become – translated the Bible into Welsh and in so doing ensured the future of the language and Welsh identity. His time spent here at Gwydir equipped him for studies at Cambridge and then the greatest task of his life. Later today I hope to find out a little more about this important figure of Welsh history.

Up the stairs now, which were built for shorter gaits and have grown uneven with age, and into the panelled parlour. In the centre of the room is a table with a white damask cloth, half-burned candlestick and a bowl of fruit. I can't resist a squeeze of the pears, assuming they must be wax and just for show – but they're the real thing and waiting for someone hungrier, perhaps one of the guests staying in the private wing through the cordoned-off door.

With a rug on the floor and tapestries lining the walls, the usual cold feel of ancient buildings is absent here. An inventory of the Great Chamber from 1627 records a comfortable existence:

> *A standing cupboard with a table and leaves, four pieces of hangings, two turkie carpets, a greene carpet with a greene silk fringe, thirteen turkie wrought cushions, 6 old turkie wrought cushions with Queene Elizabeth's name on, a crimson imbroidered chaise with two stooles belonging to it, a needle work chair, four wooden chairs, sea pictures and a map.*

The architecture of Gwydir is a hotchpotch of centuries – it's likely that Sir Charles Barry, the eminent nineteenth-century architect and designer of the new Palace of Westminster, even had a hand in its later improvements. Its building materials too came from a variety of sources. When Maenan Abbey, an important Cistercian foundation just three miles away, was demolished, the Wynn family (owners of

MOST HAUNTED IN WALES

Gwydir Castle is said to be one of the most haunted houses in Wales. The best-known ghost is that of a young woman in either white or grey who patrols certain passageways, always accompanied by a smell of putrefaction. Even those who haven't seen the ghost herself have spoken of a sudden drop in temperature and a sense of something being present. An article published in 1906 attempted to clear up the story behind this apparition, explaining that it was the result of a murder committed by Sir John Wynn in around 1700. He seduced a serving maid at Gwydir in his youth and when the relationship became tricky, Sir John murdered the girl and had her body walled up, possibly in a disused chimneybreast or a priest hole at the end of the passage by the bedroom latrines. Not surprisingly the smell of her decomposing body stuck around.

She is not the only ghost, however. Others have seen a monk who was supposedly trapped in a tunnel leading from a secret room (what was a monk doing there anyway?), and others have seen the ghost of murderous Sir John himself. As if that wasn't enough, children have been heard crying, a ghostly procession has been witnessed on the Great Terrace, and – best of all – there is supposedly a Ghost Dog. This last was eerily supported by the discovery in 1995 of a dog's skeleton in the cellar...

Gwydir at the time) made sure its dressed stone and carvings (some of them late thirteenth century) found their way here, including the spiral staircase. The desire for a retro look is nothing new.

In every room there is an air of picturesque distress. The squab cushions of the chairs are worn from generations of thighs; the floors have a few leaves blown in from the windows waiting to be swept. The tapestries have seen better centuries but this is Gwydir's great gift: the restoration of an historic country house that makes you believe that you are entering a living home – which of course it is. It would be a shame if it had been tidied up too much.

The restoration is a work in progress. The completed rooms – for example, the Blue Bedroom, its four-poster bed lying comfortably in the middle of its blue walls – offer a delightful insight into how the wealthy Welsh would have lived and worked. That there are completed rooms to enjoy is entirely due to the tireless detective work and restoration of Judy Corbett and Peter Welford, the castle's current owners. In 1921 the castle was sold and its contents scattered to the four winds. In a story that you couldn't make up, the 1640s wood panelling, doors and fireplaces were bought by the American newspaper mogul, William Randolph Hearst. The Metropolitan Museum of Art in New York bought these fittings from Hearst in 1956, and there they remained, unopened in packing cases, until they were all brought back to Gwydir after a 70-year American exile.

The search for other contents will continue until the castle is put back together, but there is an indestructibility and romance at the very heart of the place that dispersal and even fire can't extinguish. One of the Welfords' predecessors at Gwydir was the eccentric Sir Owen Wynne, who spent many of his hours trying to turn base metal into gold. In their way his British eccentricity lives on in Judy and Peter's restoration drama, which is delivering gold to lovers of Welsh history.

It's time for me to leave now, and in the ground-floor rooms the entrance bell rings again and again as more visitors join the handful wandering the grounds. Gwydir will never find itself on the tour bus route – it's too small to cope with hundreds of trippers – but for the few who find themselves tootling along the B-roads of the Conwy Valley, it's a rich treasure.

 *Betws-y-coed*

A few miles down the road the B5106 comes to a glorious end in Betws-y-coed. This is one of those rare Welsh towns where the pedestrians still rule the roads. It's high season and a honey pot for tourists – mostly walkers this morning, too numerous to be contained on the narrow pavements. Four stunningly beautiful forested river valleys meet here, and it's their rivers that produce the dramatic attractions like Swallow Falls and the mysterious Fairy Glen which both drew an artist's colony here in 1868. Many of the fine Victorian buildings still provide accommodation for today's adventurers tackling the Snowdonia National Park.

Some visitors come here to see what is unfairly described as Ugly House. According to local legend, this house was built by two outlaw brothers in a single night – a feat that, under Welsh law, entitled them to the freehold of the land. Looking at it today, it's hard to believe the story, and in fact it's more likely that the house we see was built by navvies working on Telford's London–Holyhead road who were sick of camping. Either way, it doesn't look as if there were ever any architect's plans.

Coachloads and carloads of tourists swarm over the streets; the more sedentary are drawn to the railway and motor museum. But I'm going to have to get going again. Great as it is to see the town so busy – which is wonderful for the shopkeepers, who are doing a roaring trade – it's not in the spirit of my quiet escape from the masses via the B-roads. Besides, I can't park anywhere.

On the other side of Betws-y-coed on the A5 to Pentrefoelas, the turning for the B4406 leads you onto a mountainous road and back in time to one of the landmarks of Welsh history. It takes an age to get to my destination, and as I've never been here before a sense of uncertainty begins to seize my mind – could I have taken a wrong turn? However, the winding lanes, thick woods and steep hills better suited to horseback than cars are all a part of what I'm about to see. The journey to get there is gradually taking me back in time: this is what even estate agents would call the back of beyond. At the top of the hill as the road climbs back up from the valley, all you can see in any direction is the gentle rolling landscape of untouched Snowdonia. No cars, no people, no development. It's often said that Britain is a crowded island. They clearly haven't been here. This is as far away from the madding crowd as it's possible to get without actually going mad.

Ty Mawr Wybrnant

A cottage sits in a valley shielded from the worst of the winter winds by the mountains. It's a handsome home, with stone walls under a slate roof; modest and of small proportions, it has perhaps two small rooms downstairs and two above. Smoke is curling from one of the chimneys, which leans to one side as though the whole place is made from marzipan.

This is Ty Mawr Wybrnant, set in the heart of the Conwy Valley, the birthplace in 1545 of William Morgan, the second son of five children. It's

This house, with its crooked chimney, was the birthplace of one of Wales's most important sons: William Morgan.

no exaggeration to say that if it hadn't been for the little boy born here and his later work, the story of Wales and the Welsh might have been very different. The house has been much rebuilt and remodelled over the centuries, but it's generally accepted that Morgan lived in a house on this site and that the cottage still has parts that were here in his time. It was from here that Morgan would leave for classes at Gwydir Castle. Then, at the age of 20 he went up to St John's College, Cambridge, where he remained for several years studying Hebrew and Greek – all of which came in useful for his later translations of the scriptures into Welsh.

Inside the door there is darkness for a moment until your eyes adjust to the light and the smoke that fills much of the ground floor. Wil Edwards is the curator, a bushy-moustached man of squat build. He's sitting reading at a desk behind the door, deep in thought. When he notices a visitor approaching he breaks into a welcome that almost suggests he'd been expecting you.

Ty Mawr Wybrnant is one of the smallest historic houses in Wales. It's well off the beaten track and understandably has few visitors compared with the castles and country houses. But for all that, this is worth seeking out just for the curator's enthusiasm.

Many guides to historic sites exhibit a restrained understatement born of too many retellings of the same story, but Wil is evangelical in his enthusiasm and energy. His performance of the story of this place is perhaps the best history lesson I have ever had. He drops off into Welsh occasionally as the excitement of the tale overtakes him, and moves around the room swapping places with the smoke, his face half lit from the sunlight through a shutter. The house may be tiny but his performance is truly epic. If only he could teach history in every school in the land.

The criss-cross climb over the hills to get here belies the fact that this house was once on the main drover's route from Anglesey to London, one of Britain's superhighways. The men who lived here and spent half of their lives driving their cattle to market were not poor Welsh farmers but well-travelled men of land and means. This was the home of relatively wealthy people. The cottage

THE WELSH BIBLE

Why is Morgan's Welsh Bible so significant to the history of Wales? In 1538 Henry VIII had ordered English-only Bibles to be used in Wales – this decree continued in force under the reign of Elizabeth I. It was inevitable that in civil and church life the Welsh language would slowly wither and die within a few generations and all at the hands of the state.

Morgan's translation, which was first published in 1588, ensured the Welsh language continued to have an important and honoured place in everyday spiritual life in a country that was then very devout. The work was also a substantial literary hit and so well written in accessible contemporary Welsh that it lasted for centuries after its publication – even the new text in 1988 owed much to Morgan's translation. Is it an exaggeration to say that modern Wales owes Morgan's Bible a great debt? Probably not. Without a vibrant Welsh language kept alight by the bishop's work, Wales would have lived up to the old *Encyclopedia Britannica* entry, 'For Wales, see England' and have become completely assimilated by its neighbour – it would be just another Devon or Herefordshire. Cardiff may be the capital of the country, but the heart of modern Wales lies in part in this lonely farmhouse on the edge of Snowdonia.

would have begun its life as a single-storey dwelling – one half for the family, the other for livestock. Accumulated wealth added another floor and higher rooms than the stooping space beneath. There is no glass in the windows on the ground floor – the shutters keep out the worst of the weather and the crescent-shaped, high-backed wooden settle was the next line of defence in the battle to keep warm. The Bible box on a table in one corner would have possessed the only lock on the premises, with a key for both husband and wife. There too were kept the family's documents.

The interior of Ty Mawr Wybrnant may seem modest, but was actually relatively well furnished for the sixteenth century.

My eyes are still streaming from the smoke coming from the enormous fireplace where four logs are smouldering. To one side of the fire an iron crane holds a cauldron ready to swing over the heat and begin cooking. The diet in houses like this would have been monotonous. Some meat of course – mutton, beef, pork, veal and bacon, which was either boiled or roasted on a spit and then strung out over a week – but it was oatmeal that formed the basis of a relatively well-off farmer's diet. Oatcakes, barley and rye bread would have been cooked on a bake stone at the side of the fire. Breakfast and supper would have consisted of oatmeal, while dinner would have been boiled meat and vegetables thickened with yet more oatmeal – washed down with spring water or homebrew beer.

There is a single chair at the hearth – not very comfortable-looking but substantial and at least close to the heat. At the opposite end of the room, a steep wooden staircase paired with a rope affixed to the wall offers a precarious climb upstairs. Underneath the staircase there's a cupboard in three parts – the bottom draw given as a gift on engagement (from which the phrase 'bottom drawer' comes), the middle section given on marriage and the top given on the occasion of the birth of the first child. To the side of this, next to the door, a spinning wheel to make the family's few clothes and beyond it the stable door which kept the cattle (if not their smell) from entering the parlour.

Upstairs is a box bed. The white walls have a door in the wall beside the chimneybreast – this is where meat and fish could be hung over the smoke to preserve them.

Judging by the evidence of wills and inventories from the time this house was built, up to a quarter of the dwellings in this part of Snowdonia might not have had any bedsteads, the occupants instead sleeping on straw on the floor. Over half of the local households possessed no table, while nine out of ten may not have had any chairs and used benches and stools instead. Even a comparatively wealthy house like Ty Mawr Wybrnant wouldn't have had the Welsh dresser and grandfather clock that we so associate with Welsh domestic rural life in these parts. This was a spartan life without the trappings and detritus that clutter homes today. These people lived by the doctrine of minimalism long before house makeover programmes thought it was the next big thing.

Dolwyddelan Castle

As I drive back over the hills from Penmachno to Betws-y-coed, Dolwyddelan Castle looms into view. One of the mountain strongholds of the Welsh princes, from a defensive point of view its location is superb. From there it could keep a close eye on all the comings and goings on the mountain passes of Snowdonia.

If Hollywood ever decides to film a blockbuster on the history of Wales, this would be one of the key locations. The bleakest of ruined towers sits centre stage, surrounded for miles in every direction by the cruel slopes of Snowdonia and a thousand hideouts. All that's needed is a cast of hundreds to play the brave Welsh defending the Welshest of castles as they struggle to maintain their proud independence.

The castle and the mountains were made for each other. Only a forlorn-looking romantic ruin could actually improve upon the peerless rugged landscape of Snowdonia, and Dolwyddelan's lonely beauty fits the bill perfectly. That it's here at all is a minor miracle – the castles of the native Welsh princes were most often razed to the ground.

Dolwyddelan Castle, along with Dolbadarn and Prysor, formed a collection of strategically important mountain fortresses for Llywelyn the Great (1173–1240). His grandson Llywelyn (the Last) took over the stronghold and managed to keep Edward's English forces at bay – for a while at least. It's a steep climb up the hill to the top, and I have to share the path with dozens of inquisitive sheep. There's no furniture inside – it's just me, the ghosts, the stones and my imagination. With a little assistance from Victorian restorers it remains one of the most beautiful ruins in North Wales.

Blaenau Ffestiniog

The lush green mountains and valleys of Snowdonia stop abruptly as you drop down into Blaenau Ffestiniog. The almost spiritual reverence for the landscape that I've seen so far today simply comes to an end here as the pastures part to show gashes in the hills where slate miners have gouged out the

Blaenau Ffestiniog in 1901,
*when it still lay at the heart
of slate production.*

mountains. This is the slate town that roofed the houses, town halls, hospitals and schools of an empire, and supplied windowsills, door steps and hearths around the world. As I drop down the gears on the meandering spiral that takes me to the town, I can't help thinking I'm on the set of a James Bond film and that one of the baddies will at any moment emerge from one of these tunnels.

Blaenau Ffestiniog developed in the mid-nineteenth century as a slate-mining town and by the beginning of the twentieth century 4,000 of its inhabitants were quarrymen. Today a tiny fraction of that number still work in slate, causing the town to reinvent itself. Now, visitors come here to explore the depths of the Llechwedd Slate Caverns and take a journey deep into the earth on the 1846 tram; like Big Pit, the coalmine-turned-successful tourist attraction in Blaenafon, the future for Blaenau Ffestiniog lies in taking children down the old slate mines to see how their forebears would have been working in the dripping candlelight rather than sitting their GCSEs. The underground landscape with its own lakes should be on the itinerary of those who reminisce about 'the good old days'. But as a travel writer on the *Boston Globe* once remarked, 'a gorgeous place it is not'.

Gorgeous or otherwise, Blaenau Ffestiniog provides an enormous chapter in the history of the Industrial Revolution and the story of the British Empire. You can be offended by the ugliness of the coalmines of South Wales and the slate quarries of the north and you can be appalled by the conditions in which men, women and children were exploited too. But what is beyond doubt is that places like Blaenau Ffestiniog forged the culture and experience of a people – good and bad – and were the making of a nation. Modern Wales is shaped by the legacy of these places: the mutual dependence of skilled people working together in difficult, dangerous conditions and the support of the community when it was most needed. Those values, galvanized in communities like this and in the gatherings in chapels and cabans, reading rooms and working men's clubs, changed British politics.

My journey around the B-roads of Snowdonia now takes me towards the sea in the footsteps of someone who, like the slate miners of Blaenau Ffestiniog, changed the landscape of Wales. He didn't move the mountains or mine the hills, but his work is immediately recognizable as the face of Wales around the world. Disciples of the architect Clough Williams-Ellis flock to the estuary at Portmeirion, the Italianate village immortalized in the television series *The Prisoner*. But before you get to his showpiece on the Welsh coast, some clever map-reading of the back roads leads to his ancestral home, Plas Brondanw, and the garden that, along with Portmeirion, was his life's love.

The B4410 is the best stretch in a triangular route of lanes that seems hell-bent on losing you in the Snowdonia countryside. The back road to Plas Brondanw takes you through a mountain wilderness pretty much unchanged since the great man chugged along here decades ago. There are no other cars, the track is not much wider than my wing mirrors and you'll have to stop on your way to open the various farm gates that attempt to keep in wandering sheep.

Wild Snowdonia in its all widescreen beauty is heart-stoppingly epic on a warm August day and unspeakably cruel in winter. This is the Britain that people think has long disappeared, the countryside yearned for in a thousand urban sighs. Purple heather, pink campions and yellow gorse hold the hedges together and punctuate grey stones with a dash of colour to cheer up the impenetrable forests that begin at the roadside and never seem to end.

The landscape must have had an incredible impact on Clough Williams-Ellis as he drove up and down these country lanes. Throughout his life his mission was to demonstrate that the development of a naturally beautiful site need not lead to its defilement and that good architectural manners could be good business.

Plas Brondanw

Plas Brondanw was built by Clough's distant ancestor John ap Howel around 1550. Clough was given the house by his father in 1908, at the age of 25. The house has never been bought or sold. The old house and the creation of its garden were his abiding interests outside the architectural profession.

THE BEAUTY OF B-ROADS

*A*s a strip of ancient, potholed tarmac, the average B-road is not a thing of great beauty. It's a serviceable utilitarian track, unremarkable and taken for granted. But here in Snowdonia, the B-roads **are** a thing of beauty. There's a lane, just off the B4410, whose route is as ancient as the streams flowing around it: it began life as a muddy footpath, worn into the grass by feet and hooves. Then in middle age it was fattened to carry the wider traffic of carts and their wheels. Then finally the road builders covered ancient stones and ruts with a layer of thin tarmac, the motorist's friend. As with a great painting, the frame is critical, and here the low stone walls on either side shoulder a work of art. Who could stop at the side of a motorway and admire its beauty?

Yet these dry stone walls, each yard placed by hand, have in the passing of the years acquired a patina and an organic life of their own. New roads are built by machines in flawless lines – constructed from the same material and designed to identical specification whether they are laid in Devon or Dundee – but this lane's creators took as their starting point the bequest of history, its route and its contours. Like regional accents, in every part of the country the character of the B-roads and back lanes changes: in Pembrokeshire the weak, porous stone is supplemented in farm walls with earth and planted with grass to make a boundary known as the 'Pembrokeshire hedge'. Here in Snowdonia the stone is like iron and has no need of supplements, so is piled upon itself unadorned by soil or cement.

The peaceful grounds of Plas Brondanw proved a lovely spot to sit and capture a few thoughts.

'It was for Brondanw's sake that I worked and stinted,' he wrote, 'for its sake that I chiefly hoped to prosper. A cheque of ten pounds would come in and I would order yew hedging to that extent, a cheque for twenty and I would pave a piece of terrace.' In 1951, Plas caught fire and the blaze raged through the old house with frightening speed, feeding on old timbers, panelling and partitions. By mid-morning the next day nothing remained but the three-foot-thick stone walls. Even Clough's spectacles and false teeth had perished along with all of his valuables and papers. Reconstruction took two years.

The garden is open this afternoon and there's an honesty box behind the gate (visitors to gardens never cheat, I've noticed, they're an upstanding lot). As I walk in I'm immediately struck by how beautifully the paradise in the foreground complements the surrounding mountain landscape. The generous strip of land in front of the house is divided into garden 'rooms' where hedging makes the walls and bright borders or fountains sit in place of carpet. There is nothing in the garden that has been left to chance or nature – what is there has been carefully planted for effect.

In a far corner two gardeners shout to each other in Welsh across a huge border. For them this is just another day's work in the unceasing circle of seasonal tasks. But for the half a dozen visitors wandering the grounds they are the Eden makers, the builders of paradise. Here fashioned in topiary and trees is a vision of the idealized countryside that Portmeirion would aspire to in brick

ABOVE: *The well-kept gardens of Plas Brondanw.*

OVERLEAF: *Portmeirion, with its gaily coloured buildings in a light Italianate style, has captivated visitors for the best part of a century.*

and stone. The games played with perspective and scale a few miles down the road are all employed here in lawn and hedge.

Three ladies of advancing years are wandering around. They have come here on a day out from Anglesey especially to see the garden. It's a well-kept secret shared only it seems by the horticultural and architectural cognoscenti. One of the gardeners climbs an extension ladder and with ear defenders on his head begins trimming the top of the topiary with a chain saw. With a speed that belies their age the three ladies who were walking nearby move fast to the other end of the garden to escape the scream of the two-stroke motor.

The gardener comes down from his ladder after one tree is scalped. He's worked here for years and is as passionate about the place as Clough was. He tells me that Clough, one of the founding fathers of the Snowdonia National Park, was insistent that when the boundaries were drawn (with all the restrictions on development that entailed) Plas Brondanw should be included in the Park to protect its surrounding landscape but Portmeiron, his work in progress, should be omitted to allow him to continue building!

Although not as well known as his creation at Portmeirion, the garden here at Plas Brondanw is considered by many to be Clough's most important creation. It is an insight into the mind and the private life of a very public figure and well worth a diversion to enjoy the hors-d'oeuvre before the feast that is Portmeirion.

Portmeirion

My arrival at Portmeirion is feted with hydrangeas along the drive before my progress comes to a halt at a sentry box. A man asks my business before raising the barrier and letting me pass. The location of the village is stunning. It's perched high up on the hill overlooking the estuary. The entrance at the hotel gates is all very theatrical and owes much to the TV series *The Prisoner*, which catapulted Portmeirion to international attention. The tide is coming in and you'd be forgiven for thinking that the speed with which it seems to cover such a vast tract of sand is just another piece of artistic trickery.

If the location wasn't breathtaking enough, the architecture is plucked from the realms of fantasy. The tower, dome, town houses and cottages could have been stolen from a Mediterranean hillside were it not for the Welsh dragon fluttering limply from the flagpole. Outside the entrance door, an enormous gull-wing American car from the 1950s has broken down and is causing the staff a little disquiet. There are no classic American car parts to be easily found in Porthmadog this late in the afternoon.

The duty porter arrives out of thin air and greets me with long-lost familiarity even though we've never met before. The hall is chattering with Americans, Italians and Welsh like an international operatic contest. Through the windows to the estuary I see the mast of a ship concreted to the wall and sailing nowhere, as much a part of the hotel as its roof and its walls.

Clough bought the land Portmeirion is built on in 1925 for less than 5000 pounds; the first article outlining his plans (to impress potential investors) was published a year later. Writing in the *Architects' Journal*, John Rothenstein set out what he believed to be Clough's vision: 'His scheme…should do much to shake the current notion that although houses must be designed with due care, towns may grow by chance.' Portmeirion was built in two stages, from 1925 to 1939 then from 1954 to 1976. Several of the buildings were salvaged from demolition sites, giving rise to Clough's description of Portmeirion as 'a home for fallen buildings'. Since his heyday the architectural profession in Britain

Portmeirion at low tide.

CELEBRITIES BY THE SEA

Portmeirion has always attracted more than its fair share of stars. Nöel Coward hung out here enjoying a drink on the terrace and watching his fellow diners. **Blithe Spirit** *was penned overlooking the estuary. They sang happy birthday here to George Harrison at Portmeirion on his fiftieth; Larry Adler gave an impromptu performance and Ingrid Bergman could be heard talking films with Bertrand Russell (I'd have liked to have eavesdropped on that conversation...). On the right day you might have bumped into anyone from Edward VIII to King Zog of Albania, all briefly escaping from the real world.*

The stellar list of visitors was drawn by the fairy-tale atmosphere, but also by the magnetic personality of Portmeirion's creator. Clough was one of the most fascinating creatures of his time. He was eventually knighted at the age of 90 after a distinguished career that was remarkable as much for the commissions he accepted as those he declined – after all, he turned down the tempting offer to become Stalin's town planner.

has at times fallen from public esteem. Perhaps architects forgot Clough's fight for beauty – what he described as 'that strange necessity'.

The Times called Portmeirion 'the last folly of the Western World', while the *Guardian* saw it as 'a giant gnome's village'. For Clough, it was what he called 'propaganda for the seemliness', a statement of how tourism could enhance rather than destroy the environment. For the quarter of a million visitors each year who make the trip to this corner of Wales, it is the most magical place on earth.

Sandwiches are being served at the hotel to the delight of a collection of Miss Marples, who look most at home in their comfortable surroundings. On the far shore just above the high tide, a pall of smoke from a steam locomotive hangs idly in the air. The shimmering grey-blue of the sea breaks up gently as the tide goes out, and then is parted with sandbanks lifting up like beaching whales drying their brown skin.

In the central square of Portmeirion a wedding reception is taking place. The bride, groom and guests dressed in formal wear and spectacular gowns mingle with visitors in shorts and T-shirts. The unreal world that is Portmeirion takes on yet another coat of unreality – the tourists marvelling at the Piazza can't be sure if the costumed drama is part of the attraction. An exasperated photographer with a strong North Walian accent stands precariously on a chair and begs his subjects to move left or right. Passers-by dreamily drinking in the sights obediently turn around before realizing that the orders aren't directed at them.

There are no cars in the Piazza. Despite living through the ascendancy of the motoring age, Clough realized their domination would ruin his paradise and made no provision for vehicles in his village. Instead it's the domain of the walker and resounds to the squeals of children whose parents have no need to call them back.

Beneath the tower and dome and near the ship that never sails, the last great illusion of Portmeirion is not by the hand of its great designer Clough Williams-Ellis but from the Health and Safety Executive. The hotel swimming pool that looks so deep has been made shallower at their request, no doubt so swimmers will be safer when they dive in. You can't help thinking the great architect might have silently raised his eyes to heaven, thanked the Lord he wasn't building today and then laughed.

Chapter Eight

The Path to Snowdon

LLANBERIS ◉ THE SUMMIT

*I*T'S EARLY MORNING, and Llanberis is slowly waking to the first climbers of the day. As a breed, climbers are early risers, keen to make the best of the morning in case the weather turns. The boards are already outside the cafés and pubs offering FULL WELSH BREAKFAST and UNLIMITED TEA – never coffee for a climber. After fuelling up with the kind of meal frowned upon in more sedentary circles they'll make a final visit to the outdoor shops to buy spare laces or a perhaps a new waterproof.

OPPOSITE: The summit of Snowdon, one of the crowning glories of Wales.

The mass of walkers and climbers who have come for Snowdon have replaced the hordes of quarrymen in Llanberis who would once have lived in barracks during the working week and walked home after the Saturday shift. The slate industry in Llanberis was dominated by the Dinorwig Quarry on Elidir Mountain, now a museum to what was once here. They've done a good job of recreating the conditions in which miners lived and worked, but you can never recreate the political debates, religious argument and literature discussion for which the cabans were renowned.

The natural wilderness that will draw hundreds of visitors here today is in fact anything but natural; rather, it's the product of human endeavour over generations. Thousands of years ago man cut down the trees to begin his domination of the mountain. Ancient byways, stone enclosures, holy sites and mining have all left their mark on the slopes. Sheep farming has encouraged the present cover of grass, heather and bracken, but it's not what was there before the relatively recent demand to feed large populations. It's only the natural woodland of the valleys and lowlands that truly reflect the ancient landscape of Snowdonia – though at last the replanting of more diverse and indigenous trees is slowly rebalancing the hills, too.

It's coke and smoke that catches your lungs when you arrive in Llanberis – as well as the frying bacon and sausages. The men on the steam railway are always up before the climbers, oiling up and starting fires as the kettle comes to the boil. The acrid yellow fug is unfamiliar to us now, but the older passengers and train-spotters on the platform are nostalgic for the reek once so much part of many towns. Built in 1896, this is Britain's only public narrow-gauge rack-and-pinion

railway. Its maximum gradient is 1 in 5 and it takes about two-and-a-half hours to chug up to the top of Snowdon and back, including half an hour on the summit. But I won't be among its passengers.

I stop for a moment on the lower slopes to take in the wonderful views – and catch my breath!

The car park is beginning to fill with the visitors who refuse to take the train but instead will rely on their legs to get them to the summit (although I bet a fair few will get the train back down). They are a healthy-looking bunch – young and old – many with children for whom today will be remembered for a long time to come. The sunniest day of the year won't be spent on the beaches but instead scaling the highest

mountain in England and Wales. Climbers gather around their cars and hop about as socks are swapped for something thicker, trainers exchanged for walking boots and cameras, mobile phones and water bottles are stuffed into rucksacks.

The Llanberis Path leads from the smoking locomotives sitting in the station at the bottom of the valley right to the top of Snowdon. There's no gentle introduction to the climb, it begins steep and the complaints from the first-timers surprised by its gradient echo back down the hill. At first the path winds steeply up a tarmac lane, past the Coed Victoria forestry plantation, then towards the railway's viaduct – at which point all but the heartiest early walkers pause for a breather. At the gate half a dozen walkers will pretend to stop to admire the view back towards Llanberis Pass, Llyn Padarn and the old slate quarry. Some will even wait for the crowd to pass and then call it a day. It's a steep start that at least acts as a gentle warning to less determined mountaineers. A little boy holding heavily onto his mother asks her if this is halfway yet – this will be a long day for both of them if they make it to the top.

It's five miles from here to the summit of Snowdon – not an easy flat five miles but a long, steep, slow five miles. It's been dry for a week and the earth is baked and hard. In winter, the upper reaches would be treacherous on a bad day and off limits even to the most experienced. It's a day's walk at a leisurely pace up the mountain and then back down again. When George Borrow came here in 1854 he arrived by pony and trap from Bangor, climbed to the summit and returned by pony and trap to Bangor all in the same day – it must have been a long day or a very fast pony.

Past the ruins of ancient cottages now, their wooden roofs and windows rotted deep in the earth. All that remains to tell the story of what was once here is the ring of stones and some slates where a family who once called this home are now long gone. Soon the walls and chimneybreast will rejoin the ground from where they were hewn.

ROUTES TO THE SUMMIT

*T*he Llanberis Path, which I'm taking, is the easiest, the longest and the most popular of the handful of routes up the mountain and it's more or less in earshot of the railway until the last few hundred yards of the summit. It begins with the smooth tarmac of the Llanberis lane, but it's soon replaced by rocks and boulders of varying size. The path remains uneven for the rest of the route. Even on the gentlest route this is no place for trainers and flip-flops – sturdy walking boots are essential.

The toughest way up is via Crib Goch. This knife-thin ridge or arête is particularly challenging, and not recommended for sufferers of vertigo due to the steep drops on either side. Perhaps the most famous way up, among serious walkers and scramblers at least, is the Miners' Track, previously used by copper miners. Whichever path you choose, make sure you pack well, and treat this raw nature with the respect it deserves.

A vintage photograph of Llanberis Pass.

Through the gate where a sign pinned to the crossbar warns dog-owners to keep their animals on leads during the lambing season – which is long past – I stop to look behind me; I can see Llanberis and Llyn Padarn and above them the terraces cut into the mountain to blast out the slate. On the horizon stands the large cliff of Clogwyn Du'r Arddu, then to its right the peaks of Moel Cynghorion, Foel Goch, Foel Gron and Moel Eilio, lined up like skittles in a bowling alley.

The National Parks are curious places, the custodians of the country's green spaces but also the surprising home of unlikely bedfellows. Inside Elidir Mountain, in one of Europe's largest man-made caverns, is Dinorwig Power Station. This is where you will find the hydroelectric generator relied upon for instant response when we all simultaneously put the kettle on during a commercial break. During off-peak hours electricity is used to pump water (of which there is a lot in Snowdonia) up the mountain; and in times of high demand, the same water is unleashed to generate a quick burst of electricity.

Travelling in the same haphazard fashion (though in the opposite direction), the water from the top of the mountains is my constant companion. As I struggle breathlessly upwards, it trickles past me, always finding the easiest path. Even on the driest day after weeks without rain there is always water here, sure of the way to the lake below.

This is the largest of the three Welsh National Parks, 823 square miles of the finest landscapes in Britain. Remarkably, this vast area is home to just 25,000 people – though millions of visitors swell the population throughout the year. It's a tough balancing act governing a National Park that is not the landowner but the authority responsible for safeguarding treasured countryside without curtailing farming or much-needed jobs.

A couple of runners race past the dozen or so walkers spread out in front of me who left Llanberis at the same time. Their mountain ascent will take little more than an hour before the run back down. I can't begin to imagine the level of fitness required to run up a mountain, and judging by the astonished faces in front of me who look up for a moment from the red-earthed path, I'm not alone.

Even in this wild place, this national park and all of its acres of mountain terrain, you never feel alone. This path doesn't offer the isolation and wilderness of some of the other routes – it may be the longest route but it is also the easiest, and anyone walking up this way can expect to share the experience with hundreds of others, all just as keen to get to the top. This is the National Park on one of its busiest days of summer, thronging with climbers and railway passengers. It's the precarious

MOUNTAIN RESCUE

For all its breathtaking beauty even on a clear sunny day like this, someone walking up or down Snowdon can twist their ankle, fall from the path or have a heart attack from the exertion. If in view or in company their chances of being plucked off the mountain are good, but if alone and on one of the deserted slopes away from the crowds things are more serious. Just as seaside resorts have their summer boating accidents, here the sheer scale of visitors means that accidents are inevitable. The mountain's benign look beneath the sunshine belies a cold heart.

If you get into trouble the people to call are the Llanberis Mountain Rescue Team. This organization is staffed entirely by volunteers – among their ranks you will find teachers, plumbers and doctors, as well as mountain guides. They respond to about 90 incidents every year (though that figure is rising annually).

industrialization of nature, but without the visitors Snowdonia would be poor. To be entirely alone with the mountain you'd have to come here on a weekday in winter and risk dangerous weather and low visibility. I've climbed Snowdon in those conditions and have to admit there is a certain thrill in standing on the summit in the screaming fury of wild nature, but it's also a shame not to be able to look down and see the map-like landscape of North Wales spread beneath you.

ABOVE: *Watching walkers and the train head for Snowdon's summit.*

OVERLEAF: *Snowdonia in winter: desolate, beautiful and treacherous.*

Now I pass through the tight pedestrian tunnel that ducks under the railway line. The silence of the hills is punctuated every now and then by the shrill whistles of locomotives arriving or departing higher and lower on the slopes. Even the children who shouted and screamed and ran around at Llanberis are quiet now, their copious energies channelled into one foot after another and getting to the top. No more questions about how long or how much further – from now their eyes are fixed on the path and the stones.

Looking up the valley I can see Moel Hebog in the distance towering over Bwlch Cwmbrwynog, the pass between Clogwyn Du'r Arddu and Moel Cynghorion. Legend has it that if a person should spend the night under Maen Du'r Arddu, the huge rock in the valley to the right of Clogwyn, the morning will find him either a poet or mad.

July's high rainfall has coloured the slopes deep green this summer, though early August's dry week may yet change their fashions to yellows and browns beside the constant grey.

I've now been walking for over an hour and the Halfway Café is open for tea and Welsh cakes – as well as one of the best views in Britain. There's already a small crowd waiting to reward themselves for getting this far with a sticky bun or anything else that will conjure up the energy to keep on this pilgrimage. The news that the toilet is out of order has the boys walking purposefully towards nearby rocks and the girls wishing they'd used their time in Llanberis more constructively. It's a long walk to the new summit café, perhaps an hour or two for some depending on how the gradient and tiredness take their toll.

The lady behind the counter has had a busy summer. Walkers are not interested in the recession or the euro exchange rate – they come here all year round and even in bad weather. This year there's been an extra attraction – the completion of the new summit café.

Behind the benches full of sweating walkers eating sandwiches and slowly sipping sugary tea, a half-empty green-painted train trundles down the slope, red-and-cream carriages in tow. Its metallic whine is higher pitched than the straining wheeze of the laden uphill service. This early the downhill trains are quiet, with no one yet returning from the summit; their heavily smoking uphill sisters, however, are packed.

Even if you are a regular jogger or go to the gym, walking up a mountain carrying a rucksack calls on muscles that you didn't know you had. My toes and the balls of my feet are aching painfully now after seemingly forever walking upwards, and the pinched muscles of my back below the rucksack strap start to warm and then ache after a couple of hours. The sweat soaking my shirt and dripping from my forehead finds its way into my eyes and for a moment its sweet sting hides the growing view. Even after a cup of tea in the shadow of the café I feel cold from the sweat taking hold and eager to return to the sunshine.

Perhaps I was always meant to be a train spotter – Huw never grew out of bikes either.

Despite the rising temperatures, the low cloud has been slow to shift from the distant summit. What a disappointment to have waited for a clear day only for it to be misty. However, it's early yet and there's still time for it to burn off and clear. Y Garn towards Nantlle comes into view through Bwlch Cwmbrwynog, where the path forks by a cairn. The right-hand path is the old miner's path to the disused copper mines on Clogwyn Coch – though these days its riches are the challenging crags which rock climbers hang from.

Somewhere far below in the valley a shepherd is whistling to his dog rounding up sheep. The straggle of dog owners walking in front and behind watch their animals' ears twitch at the unseen commands before snapping on their leads. The shepherd remains invisible, as does his dog, but a flock appears from nowhere and seems to round itself up, having no need of the middleman.

The path has now turned into a loose gravel track; in parts it has been repaired and replaced with large boulders that look like a Roman road. It's a constant battle to keep a route in reasonable repair given the onslaught of walkers, not to mention winter's torrents washing the stones away. It makes for uneven and hard walking, your gait erratic and unsteady, forcing you to choose your footsteps carefully. Later a little digger sits to the side of a muddy hole where the path once ran – in the autumn when the summer crowds have dispersed, the workmen will return and begin the thankless task once more.

As I walk up Snowdon, leaning forwards engrossed in the path and its surface, it's easy to forget to stop and look back at the changing panorama behind. Any excuse for a breather. The lake is far below me now and Llanberis long lost and hidden by the hill. On the other hand, far-away Anglesey has come into sight and the Irish Sea is now on the horizon, along with the long arm of the Llyn Peninsula. Far beneath and ahead strung out for a mile is the shuffling progression of a colourful pilgrimage as though heading for some venerable shrine. At this time of day we are all heading in one direction, a human elevator leaning on walking poles and snaking up the long grey gash in the hillside. Within a few hours the orderly line set on one purpose will become confused as the ascenders and descenders meet.

The ground on Allt Moses – Moses Hill – is loose and strewn with boulders. Far beneath us now is the green water of Llyn Du'r Arddu where the miners used to wash the copper ore. I'm approaching Clogwyn station, where the cheats on the train will no doubt disembark and walk the last stretch up the mountain to say they've climbed Snowdon. Cwm Glas Bach below us is known locally as Cwm Hetiau – the valley of hats – from the days when open-topped carriage passengers would lose their headgear in high winds and locals would chance upon new hats on the valley floor.

The long strides of the lower mountain have been mostly replaced by shorter and more tired steps now; similarly, the long discussions have been cut back to short questions and answers pushed out between deep breaths. Yet there is so much to talk about, to describe and share. The cloud is lifting and as it disappears I'm left with the emerging relief of the Ordnance Survey map, the lakes and mountains popping out of the flat paper and into the sky. However, there's no breath to express delight or emotion, and only energy enough to look and drink in.

The path from Bwlch Glas becomes steeper now and Llyn Cwellyn, which supplies Caernarfon with its water, looks like a brimming bowl. Walking non-stop I could probably be at the summit in about 15 minutes, but the gradient is taking its toll and the scree to the side of the path is littered with walkers sitting, taking stock and catching their breath before the final skidding assault.

The summit looks like the mountain-top castle that used to open the old Warner Brothers films, a fairy-tale fortress floating in the clouds. As we approach the last thousand yards half a dozen paths and their walkers converge on the approach to the top and swell the host. This was never going to be a solitary affair, but out of nowhere from behind ledges and peaks come hundreds of new fellow travellers all intent upon the same narrow ledge.

The name Snowdon comes from the Saxons, who spoke of the Snow Hill or fortress. However, to the ancient Welsh this place was known as Eryri – the abode of eagles (though these have long gone). The mountain's Welsh name – Yr Wyddfa, the great mound or tomb – comes from the legend that Rhita Fawr, slain by King Arthur, is buried here. Nevertheless, I suspect that most walkers here will tell their friends that they climbed Snowdon today.

There is a harsh brutality about the upper slopes of the mountain. It is forbidding and almost cruel, treeless and barren without heather or grass – even the sheep know there's little for them up this high. The forests, too, keep to the lower stretches since up here it's too wind blasted for anything very tall. Stripped of any green or purple with just stone on its slopes there is a stark beauty in its emptiness. Like a comfortless pulpit in an old church what matters is the congregation at your feet, the carpet of blue and green far below.

The huge stone cairn swarming with climbers is said to have been built by the Ordnance Surveyors making their maps; it was also once home to two large huts with bunks, where travellers could stay overnight and be fed and watered for the princely sum of ten shillings. These huts were replaced by the old summit café, which stood beneath the cairn.

The last yards are a clamber over boulders and scree alongside tired dogs and families too exhausted to be triumphant (except for those whose summit assault was completed by train – they strut unsweating to the café, after which their exertions will be complete). Those who have walked find a perch to sit and stare – for the moment they need to rest complaining muscles. The silence is broken by the conversation only of downward-bound walkers discussing routes and times – it is only they who have the energy to speak.

The very top of Snowdon isn't as quiet as it used to be – having so many visitors is something of a mixed blessing.

A man in an ill-fitting wig passes me, anxious to join the crowd of twenty standing on the very top; it must be hot wearing that. The gathering throng feels more like a rugby crowd than mountain conquerors; hundreds mill back and forth in the rubble of land between the summit and its café. Some are phoning friends and family on their mobiles; others wait patiently beneath what looks like a motorcycle display team precariously balanced on the summit for a photo to capture the great feat (along with three dozen strangers in the shot). Each takes their turn for that conquest picture, edging gingerly around strangers before finding the top spot. In front and behind the grandstand of spectators, the unfolding ripples of landscape of lakes and hills, their peaks softened by water from when they were deep under the sea.

It's lunchtime at the new summit café. The old building, designed by Clough Williams-Ellis, was past its best and the repair and maintenance bills were increasing. It had few fans in its decline, and was even described by Prince Charles as 'the highest slum in Wales'. That building and all of its ugly smelly concrete has long been demolished. The whole argument as to whether there should even be a café at the top of the mountain is a long and tortuous one. The Snowdonia Mountain Railway has carried visitors to the top since 1896 and the summit café generates £2.4 million annually for a hard-pressed local economy. Many hardy climbers say it's a desecration of the mountain, but whatever the merits or otherwise there has been a summit-top café for years and it has just been replaced by a new structure – one of my main motivations for climbing the mountain is to see it for myself after reading so much about it.

The achievement of building anything on the top of Snowdon shouldn't be underestimated. The howling vengeance of winter at the top of this mountain makes any form of activity – walking, running a railway or building a world-class architectural landmark – nothing short of miraculous. *Hafod Eryri* (to give the new building its proper name) is a beautiful piece of architecture. Covered in granite to blend in with the landscape, its curved roof doesn't interrupt the view from the summit cairn. Rainwater from its roof flushes the toilets, the large windows mean less energy is required and the majority of its raw materials were local (the foundations were very local, being made from the rubble of the old building). From the front elevation it looks like a cool lair from which to attempt world domination.

The inside of the café has the initial appearance of a sauna – three of its walls are of light wood, though that is where any comparison ends. No surface is left untouched to tell the story of the mountain. The floor is inlaid with inscriptions, and the great triumph of the interior – the glass wall looking down the mountain – offers a view that few places in the world could rival. If there are such things as views in heaven they would be hard pushed to match this – on a clear day you can see all the way to the coast.

When Thomas Pennant came here writing his *Tours of Wales* in 1784 he was less fortunate: 'The sky was obscured very soon after I got up. A vast mist enveloped the whole circuit of the mountain. The prospect down was horrible. It gave the idea of numbers of abysses, concealed by thick smoke, furiously circulating about us. Very often a gust of wind formed an opening in the clouds, which gave a fine and distinct vista of lake and valley…exhibiting a most strange and perplexing sight of waters, fields, rocks or chasm. They closed at once and left us involved in total darkness.'

What is less heavenly is the painfully long queue for food and drink. The café's staff seem to have been taken by surprise by the amount of people who wanted to climb the mountain on a sunny August day. Supplies of everything are running low and the tables remain cluttered with plastic trays, used water bottles, paper cups and dozens of bits of packaging from countless lunches. It's like a scene from Gatwick Airport after a Greek air traffic controllers' strike. The fare is mountaineering food, the stuff to give you energy after a long climb, lots of carbohydrates: pasties and Oggies (the Welsh miners' dish of meat and potato wrapped up in pastry). In the glass by my seat the words of the great writer Gwyn Thomas are etched: 'All around us are the grandeur and the anguish of an old, old nation.'

There isn't much anguish behind the counter. They're doing a roaring trade – half a million visitors to Snowdon every year and most of them have arrived this lunchtime. Mountain walking is big business – many of the customers in here are young affluent types who will have each swelled the county's coffers by several hundred pounds on their holiday. There aren't enough tables and benches so strangers sit alongside each other; some share tales of the great day, while others just watch the birds fly beneath us.

Outside the wiser walkers have brought their own sandwiches wrapped in squares of silver foil and sit away from the hubbub of the summit-top retail experience. I'm going to have another attempt at standing on the very top of the summit above the café. There is no let-up in the lines of walkers who still arrive from every direction and the dozens of railway passengers (conspicuous by their different clothes, since they seem to be dressed for a day at a shopping mall).

The group photos continue. Some are shot by strangers so the whole group can be snapped, and then the text messages accompanying the picture are typed – 'On Snowdon's summit 3559 feet and it's sunny!'

A dog let off its lead by its owner walks backwards, bewildered at the seagulls hovering beneath him and the inversion of the normal order of things. A crisp packet and sandwich wrapper roll past on the breeze. The train whistles notice of its imminent departure and a small crowd hurry

to the station in slow motion, picking their way past boulders and stones.

The crowd swarming towards the higher altar around the cairn and beside the café don't linger for long and as purposefully as they arrived begin their dispersal. Most retrace their steps down to Llanberis, others towards Crib Goch, Yr Aran or Moel Cynghorion, the quieter routes, lost in thought and scenery.

This is not an individual endeavour or a triumph of the few but an industrial number of tourists who have all made it to the summit of the highest mountain in Wales. I thought I might have been disappointed to have to share Snowdon with such a large crowd, but the sight of thousands of people walking up and down the mountain on the paths below me almost brings a lump to my throat. Most of them will never climb up here again, but as a result of this collective act of worship of the Welsh countryside by so many people I suspect that the countryside is stronger and safer today.

The shadows are lengthening now and the slopes changing shades. It is when descending the mountain that Snowdonia's epic majesty is at its most magnificent. Like an opera performed in reverse, at the summit its scenery is the view of giants – the walker's determined uphill stare at the gravel path is rewarded with a grand finale and its final flourish. On the long walk back down to Llanberis the music's soaring arias get softer until all the notes become quiet.

It is worth the climb when you see the view from the top on a clear day.

Conclusion

*I*T SEEMS wrong to try to draw profound conclusions from a relatively modest jaunt around a small country. The only thing I know for certain after spending the majority of a year of spare time on the B-roads and byways of Wales is that I want to go back and discover much more.

Yet there is no doubt that my time on the road has allowed me to see my country in a new light. Writers have been scrawling about their travels in Wales for a thousand years, most often to complain about inhospitable welcomes at inns. For a good part of those thousand years not much changed in Wales, but the last two hundred years have visited upon the landscape the most profound new order. Industrialization quite literally moved mountains as coal and steel headed through the ports to the Empire. The accompanying growth in population turned a country numbering hundreds of thousands into three million in a relatively short space of time.

This was the Wales of my grandparents' and parents' generation, an essential yet marginalized corner of Britain. The twentieth century did at least bring radio and television, which in turn allowed a dormant sense of Welsh identity to re-emerge. These modern tools of communication breathed new life into an ancient dying language and restored a long-lost sense of national pride. Without this, there is every possibility that Wales might have ended up as culturally indistinct as a county such as Hampshire (no offence to Hampshire).

Yet beyond the ancient rivalry with England and the challenges faced by a post-industrial economy, to my mind the greatest problem is our own indifference. I have visited dozens of unspoilt, beautiful villages, yet I lost count of the towns where shopkeepers and their customers complained about some insensitive out-of-town development that was threatening the traditional town centre. The very communities saved from certain extinction by the protests of the 1960s, and which have just about survived the decline of traditional industries such as coal and slate, are now threatened by homogenization. The sense of community in Wales that is still talked about and envied elsewhere is under threat.

Visiting many old castles, churches and stately homes it occasionally crossed my mind that one day travellers will gawp outside former butchers and post offices, marvelling at what was once there, and consider that their demise was sad but inevitable in the unsentimental march of history. After all, former slate and coal mines have already been converted into museums. Perhaps future tourists will scratch their heads, not understanding why so many of these beautiful places were

A deserted B-road in Snowdonia.

allowed to become ghost towns, or else will be shown through interactive displays how young people had to move out of their communities in search of affordable homes or gainful employment.

One of my greatest pleasures in writing this book was finishing writing up my notes every night and walking outside for a while at whichever cottage, bed and breakfast or hotel I was staying in. If you live in a town or a city you'll know the absence of car alarms or other people's noise is a rare joy. As is the experience of complete darkness so black that you can see the night sky's treasures. If you saw a man standing looking up at the stars and silhouetted countryside beneath, it might have been me, soaking it up wide-eyed and still awed by a country that is so beautiful.

Acknowledgements

M̄Y SINCERE THANKS to Tony O'Shaughnessy and Dr John Davies who read through my raw manuscripts. Andy Davies spent many days venturing out into unreliable weather to capture the moment; his photography is a delight and his contribution to this book enormous. Mark O'Callaghan, Gail Morris Jones and Cathryn Allen turned a blind eye to my absences at the BBC. Carey Smith at Ebury Press has been an inspiration to work for – she commissioned the book and has always been an encouraging voice; my grateful appreciation goes to her and her assistant Samantha Smith and also to my editor Christopher Dell who wielded his scalpel with generous charm and great skill – no easy task but he carried it out with great aplomb. My family and friends endured months of my disappearances and cancellations over the course of a year of travels and to them my thanks for their patience and endurance. So many communities I visited were welcoming and helpful – they are too numerous to list here but they know who they are. Any mistakes that remain are mine.

Picture Credits

The publishers would like to thank the following for providing photographs and permission to reproduce copyright material. While every effort has been made to trace and acknowledge all copyright holders, we would like to apologise should there be any errors or omissions.

All images © Andy Davies apart from:

Cover and title page © Ebury Press; Corbis pages 37, 101, 118; Getty Images page 113; Hulton Archive/Getty Images page 48; Jamie Owen pages 7, 8, 16, 21, 30, 163; Mary Evans Picture Library pages 78, 82, 126, 146, 157; Mural by Rex Whistler, Plas Newydd, The Collection of the Marquess of Anglesey (on long-term loan to The National Trust) © NTPL/John Hammond, © Estate of Rex Whistler. All rights reserved, DACS 2009, page 107; © National Museum Wales/The Bridgeman Art Library page 56; Simmons Aerofilms/Science & Society Picture Library page 176; Time Life/Getty Images page 66.

Bibliography

General
Davies, J., *A History of Wales* (Allen Lane, 1993)
Davies, M., *Discovering Welsh Houses* (Graffeg, 2007)
Jenkins, S., *Wales: Churches, Houses, Castles* (Allen Lane, 2008)
Tomes, J., *Wales* (W W Norton & Co, 1995)
Tree, M., and M. Baker, *Forgotten Welsh Houses* (Hendre House Publishing, 2008)
Winn, C., *I Never Knew That About Wales* (Ebury Press, 2007)

Pembrokeshire
Goddard, T., *Pembrokeshire Shipwrecks* (Christopher Davies Publishers, 1988)
John, B., *Pembrokeshire Coast Path* (Aurum Press, 2008)
Jones, F., *Historic Houses of Pembrokeshire and Their Families* (Brawdy Books, 1996)
Wyn, H., *Battle of the Preselau 1946–1948: The Campaign to Safeguard the Sacred Pembrokeshire Hills* (Eisteddfod Maencolchog, 2008)

Cardiff
Betjeman, J., *BBC Radio Talks Cardiff Castle* (1952)

Vale of Glamorgan
Kelly, V., *St Illtud's Church, Llantwit Major* (D. Brown & Sons Ltd, 1993)
Orrin, G. R., *Mediaeval Churches of the Vale of Glamorgan* (D. Brown & Sons Ltd, 1988)

Anglesey
Beretta, C. W., *The Rex Whistler Experience at Plas Newydd* (C. W. Beretta, 2002)
National Trust, *Plas Newydd, Isle of Anglesey* (National Trust, 1988)
Taylor, A., *Beaumaris Castle* (Cadw Welsh Historic Monuments, 1999)

B-Roads to Portmeirion
Corbett, J., *Castles in the Air* (Ebury Press, 2004)
Llewelyn, R., *Portmeirion* (Gomer Press, 2005)
Welford, P., *Gwydir Castle: A Brief History and Guide* (Peter Welford, 2000)

Snowdon
Rowland, E. G., *The Ascent of Snowdon* (Cidron P, 1956)

Gazetteer

BEAUMARIS CASTLE
Castle Street, Beaumaris, Isle of Anglesey,
LL58 8AP
Tel: 01248 810361
www.cadw.wales.gov.uk/

BODYSGALLEN HALL
Llandudno, North Wales LL30 1RS
Tel: 01492 584466
www.bodysgallen.com/

CAERNARFON CASTLE
Castle Ditch Caernarfon, Gwynedd, LL55 2AY
Tel: 01286 677617
www.caernarfon-castle.co.uk/

CARDIFF AQUABUS
Tel: 02920 472004
Email: info@aquabus.co.uk
www.cardiffaquabus.com/

CARDIFF CASTLE
Castle Street, Cardiff, CF10 3RB
Tel: 029 2087 8100
Email: cardiffcastle@cardiff.gov.uk
www.cardiffcastle.com/

CARDIFF MARKET
St Mary Street, Cardiff, CF1 2AU
Tel: 029 2087 1214
www.cardiff-market.co.uk/
The Market is open Monday to Saturdays,
8am until 5.30 pm.

CONWY CASTLE
Rosehill Street, Conwy, LL32 8LD
Tel: 01492 592358
www.conwy.com/

EGLWYSBACH AGRICULTURAL AND
HORTICULTURAL SHOW
Tel: 01492 650529

GREAT ORME TRAMWAY
Victoria Station, Church Walks, Llandudno,
LL30 2NB
Tel: 01492 879306
Email: tramwayenquiries@conwy.gov.uk
www.greatormetramway.co.uk/

GWYDIR CASTLE
Llanrwst, North Wales, LL26 0PN
Tel: 01492 641687
Email: info@gwydircastle.co.uk
www.gwydircastle.co.uk/

LLANDUDNO CABLE CAR
Happy Valley, Great Orme, Llandudno
Tel: 01492 877205
www.attractionsnorthwales.co.uk/attractions/
llandudno-cable-car

OLD BEAUPRE CASTLE
www.cadw.wales.gov.uk/

PEMBROKESHIRE COAST NATIONAL PARK
Tel: 0845 345 7275
Email: info@pembrokeshirecoast.org.uk
www.pcnpa.org.uk/

PLAS BRONDANW
Croesor, Llanfrothen, Gwynedd, LL48 6SW
Tel: 01743-241181
www.brondanw.org/

PLAS LLANMIHANGEL
Llanmihangel, Near Cowbridge, Vale of
Glamorgan, South Wales, CF71 7LQ
Tel: 01446 774610
Email: plasllanmihangel@ukonline.co.uk
www.plasllanmihangel.co.uk/

PLAS NEWYDD COUNTRY HOUSE AND GARDENS
Llanfairpwll, Anglesey, LL61 6DQ
Tel: 01248 715272
www.nationaltrust.org.uk/main/w-plasnewydd

PORTMEIRION
Tel: 01766 772311 (Tollgate)
For Sat Nav use LL48 6ER
Email: info@portmeirion-village.com
www.portmeirion-village.com/

SENEDD
National Assembly for Wales
Cardiff Bay, Cardiff, CF99 1NA
Tel: 08450 105500
www.assemblywales.org/sen-home/sen-
about-senedd.htm

SNOWDON MOUNTAIN RAILWAY
Llanberis, Gwynedd, LL55 4TY
Tel: 0844 493 8120
www.snowdonrailway.co.uk/

TY MAWR COTTAGE
Penmachno, Betws y Coed, Conwy County
Tel: 01690 760213
www.walesdirectory.co.uk/tourist-
attractions/Historic_Houses/Ty_Mawr_Wybr
nant.htm

WALES MILLENNIUM CENTRE
Bute Place, Cardiff, CF10 5AL
Tel: 08700 40 2000
www.wmc.org.uk/

10 9 8 7 6 5 4 3 2 1

First published in 2010 by Ebury Press, an imprint of Ebury Publishing

A Random House Group Company

Text © Jamie Owen 2010

The Random House Group Limited Reg. No 954009

Addresses for companies within the Random House Group can be found at www.randomhouse.co.uk

A CIP catalogue record for this book is available from the British Library

Photographer: Andy Davies
Designer: David Fordham
Copyeditor and indexer: Christopher Dell
Picture researcher: Victoria Hall
Printed and bound by C & C Offset Printing Co., LTD.

ISBN: 9780091932824

To buy books by your favourite author and register for offers visit www.rbooks.co.uk

Cover and title page shows the author at Strumble Head on the Pembrokeshire Coast Path. Half title page shows Caernarfon Castle.

The train pulls out of Britain's highest railway station, just below the peak of Snowdon, heading for Llanberis.